Adventure Relativity

Also by Steve Gardiner

Devils Tower: A Climber's Guide (with Dick Guilmette)

Why I Climb: Personal Insights from Top Climbers

Under the Midnight Sun (with John Jancik)

Building Student Literacy Through Sustained Silent Reading

Highpointing for Tibet (with John Jancik)

Mountain Dreams: The Drive to Explore, Experience, and Expand

Adventure Relativity

When Intense Experience Shifts Time

───────────────────

─────────

By Steve Gardiner

Copyright 2020 by Steve Gardiner
www.quietwaterpublishing.com

ISBN-13: 978-1-947427-01-3

All rights reserved. No part of this book may be reproduced in any form without written permission of the author.

Note: The names and places in this book are factual. The events have been presented as accurately as possible based on field notes, journals, letters, interviews, and other records.

Front Cover
Steve Gardiner splashes through glacial meltwater in North Peary Land, Greenland, where he witnessed the Fata Morgana phenomenon during the American Top of the World Expedition in July 1996. Photo by Dr. Joe Sears.

Back Cover
The beautiful lakes of the Beartooth Mountains in Montana are the setting for several of the solo adventures combined into the final essay in this book. Photo by Steve Gardiner.

To Greta, Romney, and Denby
With Love

Table of Contents

Introduction: A Moment of Time in the Mind.......................11

1. A Moment of Illusion in Greenland................................15
2. A Moment of Darkness in South Dakota........................25
3. A Moment of Grandeur in the Crazy Mountains.............35
4. A Moment of Shock in Space..67
5. A Moment of Heartbreak in Jackson Hole......................79
6. A Moment of Childhood Joy in Kansas..........................95
7. A Moment of Truth in Peru..105
8. A Moment of Tumbling on Molt Hill.............................117
9. A Moment of Altitude in Argentina................................125
10. A Moment of Heat in Boston...143
11. A Moment of Terror in Tanzania...................................163
12. A Moment of Solitude in the Beartooth Mountains........211

Conclusion: A Moment of Overtime......................................229

Acknowledgements: A Moment of Thanks...........................231

About the Author...233

"I still find each day too short for
all the thoughts I want to think,
all the walks I want to take,
all the books I want to read, and
all the friends I want to see."
--John Burroughs

Introduction

A Moment of Time in the Mind
August 25, 2018

Tires screeched on the pavement. I glanced at the rear-view mirror, saw the blue pickup looming behind us, swerving to the right, and crashing into the rear of our Jeep. We heard the crunching metal, felt the blow that snapped off the right rear tire and launched the pickup into the ditch, rolling onto its top. The contact drove us forward on three wheels, the rear axle trenching the highway until I could steer us onto the shoulder.

My wife Peggy and I looked each other in disbelief. We assured ourselves that we were not injured, scrambled out of the car, and ran back to the overturned pickup. Other motorists had stopped and were helping the driver release his seat belt and climb out the side window.

We had destroyed two vehicles, but none of us was scratched. We stood in the ditch, shaking our heads over the damage, the near tragedy, and listened to the sirens approaching in the distance.

The wreck lasted three or four seconds, a fleeting instant that passes hundreds of times each day. However, the intensity of that moment changed our perception of time, and a thousand details of those seconds remain with us, trapped in our minds, long after the wreck.

Much philosophical thought and scientific inquiry have been given to human perception of time, and multiple experiments tell us that we don't have a single receptor for monitoring time. Time perception is different from our other senses of taste, smell, hearing, sight, and touch, because it is not directly perceived, but must be pieced together by a network in our brains. Our sense of seconds, minutes, days, weeks, months, and years is a combination of many factors with two of the most important being our age and our emotional state.

"Our perception of time is very revealing of our emotional state," said Sylvie Droit-Volet, professor at the Social and Cognitive Psychology Laboratory in France, speaking in *The Guardian*. "There is no single, uniform time, but rather multiple times which we experience. Our temporal distortions are a direct translation of the way in which our brain and body adapt to these multiple times, the times of life."

Like a shipwrecked sailor on an island marking days with a scratch on a rock or tree trunk, human beings learned, throughout history, how to keep track of time. We created sundials, hourglasses, clocks, watches, and calendars. Later, for convenience, we designated time zones, then learned to adjust those with Daylight Savings Time.

One of the most important lessons we learn in life is to respect time. We respect the time of others. We show up for meetings on time. We don't keep others waiting. We don't tell them boring or redundant stories.

We respect our own time. We learn to use time wisely, to not waste time. We strive to give our time meaning.

Time taken away from us makes us angry. No one likes to wait in traffic or stand in line at the airport. We seldom enjoy a hospital waiting room. Few people can sit through an unorganized presentation without squirming in their seats. We try to be patient, accepting, but anticipating a college acceptance letter or a response to a job interview can cause us to wish away time, even though our more common wish is to slow time down.

We measure any number of things using time. Many people work for pay by the hour, and some weeks collect overtime. Lawyers and accountants record billable hours in their ledgers. We pay for services from plumbers and electricians by an hourly rate. We rent cars, hotel rooms, and apartments by the day, week, or month.

We use time as a reward, such as a day off or a vacation. We use time as a punishment when we send people to prison and take away time from their freedom.

Religious leaders, psychologists, novelists, poets, and others give us advice about seizing the day, about making the most of the time we have in this life.

Even language has responded to time. We learn a long list of expressions referencing time.

"Time is ticking."
"Time is money."
"It's just a matter of time."
"Time flies."
"Only time will tell."
"In the nick of time."

We also use time in every sentence we speak. We refer to events in the past tense, the present tense, the future tense, and we make the mental adjustments necessary to move between those realms.

The word time "can function as a noun, an adjective, or a verb," wrote best-selling author Daniel Pink in his book *When*. "It is one of the most expansive and versatile words we have. 'Time' can be a proper noun, as in 'Greenwich Mean Time.' The noun form can also signify a discrete duration ('How much time is left in the second period?'), a specific moment ('What time does the bus to Narita arrive?'), an abstract notion ('Where did the time go?'), a general experience ('I'm having a good time'), a turn at doing something ('He rode the roller coaster only one time'), a historical period ('In Winston Churchill's time...'), and more. In fact, according to Oxford University Press researchers, 'time' is the most common noun in the English language."

The way that we perceive time, as moving quickly or slowly, as ceasing to exist, or as plodding steadily forward, determines much about how we view our lives. How we perceive time at any given moment frames how we organize life, and how we experience it.

Throughout a lifetime of adventure travel and intense experiences, I have found many moments where time seemed to shift. There are memories of childhood joy where time simply didn't exist. There are moments of beauty and awe where time appears to float like a leaf on a stream. There are seconds of fear during an emergency where time feels sharp, like it has claws holding us in when all we want is to get out of the situation. There are national and world events which anchor us to the fabric of historical time. There are occasions when we are alone, when we must deal with time in solitude.

In the following chapters, I recount adventures and experiences that kept me on the edge, shifting my recognition of time, challenging my senses, driving my emotions, creating lasting memories, and giving me understanding and meaning in life.

A Moment of Illusion in Greenland

Chapter 1

Real Sense Surreal
July 24, 1996

Seeing is believing.
What you see is what you get.
I saw it with my own eyes.

We are taught to believe what we see. We trust eyewitnesses in the courtroom. We perceive the truth through our senses. Our eyes give us perspective on the world.

But what happens when we doubt what we see, when we feel deceived by our sight?

Thomas Hardy, the British novelist and poet, once wrote, "There is a condition worse than blindness, and that is, seeing something that isn't there."

When that happens, we turn to those around us. "Did you see what I saw?" We want confirmation. We want to continue to trust our senses. We want to maintain our grasp of reality.

I felt that shock, that sense of illusion when I left our camp on the northern coast of Greenland to walk alone along the edge of the Arctic Ocean. Our American Top of the World Expedition had been in Greenland three weeks, exploring the small islands offshore and climbing mountains. We were taking a day off to rest. It felt great to walk by myself in such a land of beauty. To my left, the snowy mountains of the H. H. Benedict Range rose above the muddy flats of the shoreline. Ahead of me, I could see the Roosevelt Range. To my right, the sea ice of the Arctic Ocean spread out, white and vast,

The team camped on the sea ice at the mouth of Sands Fjord in North Peary Land, Greenland, on July 21, 2001. This is looking north out onto the frozen Arctic Ocean where the Fata Morgana illusion occurred. Photo by Steve Gardiner

uninterrupted for four hundred miles between me and the North Pole.

In Greenland, the July sun never sets, never even approaches the horizon. It holds the air temperature at just above freezing around the clock. That sun played with our natural patterns, our daily rhythms. Our most basic units of time, night and day, had been disrupted.

I had seen horizontal and vertical sundials, but this was a celestial sundial. It circled in the sky above us, one full circle each twenty-four hours. It changed our words. Tomorrow morning. Tomorrow night. Neither seemed to have any meaning when living under an ever-present sun.

I stepped onto the sea ice. Walking on the ocean. It seemed like a strange idea, but we had walked on the the sea ice enough that it had become comfortable to us, and we enjoyed looking down into it, seeing the designs, formed by air bubbles and wind, etched in the ice.

As I walked, my boots crunched on rough granules. When I stopped to look inside a hole in the sea ice, silence returned to the world. The air was still. We were hundreds of miles north of the nearest village. Nothing moved. Deep quiet.

Inside the icy hole, I could see water, melted in the sunlight. I could see layers of ice below. When I looked up, across the sea ice toward the north, I gasped. On the horizon was a range of crystal mountains, shining under the Arctic sun.

Interesting.

They hadn't been there yesterday.

I was not the first person to look out over the Arctic Ocean and see strange mountains. Early expeditions searching for the Northwest Passage or seeking a route to the North Pole often reported facing unknown land masses and mountains rising from the sea ice. One such expedition, in 1818 under Sir John Ross, actually turned around because Ross believed the route to the Northwest Passage, a sea route between the North Atlantic and North Pacific via the Arctic Ocean, was blocked. In 1906, Robert Peary, while scouting his eventual route to the North Pole, reported seeing a land mass and mountains at eighty-three degrees north latitude off the coast of Canada.

Many subsequent expeditions and flyovers have confirmed that no land masses exist where their reports claimed they did. Their sightings were a form of mirage, a phenomenon called Fata Morgana which may occur on land or sea, in polar regions or deserts, although the sea ice of the Arctic seems to be a particularly effective medium for producing the images.

When we see the pool of water ahead of us on an asphalt highway, the heat from the asphalt is bending the light rays and reflecting the sky on the road, taking an image from above and making it appear lower, known as an inferior mirage. Fata Morgana works in reverse. Fata Morgana occurs when there is a thermal inversion, a cooler layer of air is trapped close to the earth - or sea ice - by a warmer layer above it. When light hits the boundary between these two layers, it is bent or refracted by the differing densities of the layers. In the case of Fata Morgana, the refraction is sharp enough that the bending exceeds the curvature of the earth, making objects beyond the horizon seem to rise up and settle into a straight visual line in front of the viewer, a superior mirage. Because the light rays may be refracted in multiple places and at different angles, Fata Morgana images may appear to be stacked on top of each other. Some images may look inverted and images may even seem to move.

Some reports of Fata Morgana are based on man-made objects. For example, sailors on one ship report seeing another ship, behind the horizon, rise into the air and float above the sea. Other reports, like mine, are more likely distortions of natural objects, such as the rough edges of the sea ice projected onto the sky as ice-capped mountains.

As I stood on the northern coast of Greenland, I knew there were no mountains to the north. The sea ice stretches to the North Pole. I had seen many maps of the region. I had read countless expedition reports. Yet, as I stood there, I could see the silvery mountains rising on the horizon. The light played on their slopes. The mountains rose into the sky, appearing to be hundreds or thousands of feet tall. They stretched the full span of the skyline, filling the panorama.

I had read about Fata Morgana, had hoped that I might get the chance to see it while we were in Greenland. Then, in that instant, it was in full play in front of me. While I watched the show, I knew in my mind that there were no mountains there. I knew the peaks were perception, illusions of light, but that didn't stop me from staring, from wishing I could climb those magnificent mountains as well.

There was a wave, rising and falling in the mountains. Some peaks appeared to grow bigger, some smaller. It was a subtle flow, an earthquake motion throughout the icy range.

William Golding captured a moment like this in his 1954 novel *Lord of the Flies*. Before things went terribly wrong for the young boys on the tropical island, they settled into a peaceful, happy existence. They were eating fruit, building huts, swimming in the warm water,

When Intense Experience Shifts Time

As the Moore Glacier slides downhill, it meets the static sea ice of the Arctic Ocean, and the slow-motion collision forms these jagged shards of ice. Photo by Steve Gardiner

and playing in the sand. It was an idyllic life.

However, if they looked up from their play and out toward the water, they noticed, as Golding wrote, that "Strange things happened at midday. The glittering sea rose up, moved apart in planes of blatant impossibility; the coral reef and the few stunted palms that clung to the more elevated parts would float up into the sky, would quiver, be plucked apart, run like raindrops on a wire or be repeated as in an odd succession of mirrors. Sometimes land loomed where there was no land and flicked out like a bubble as the children watched. Piggy discounted all this learnedly as a 'mirage'; and since no boy could reach even the reef over the stretch of water where the snapping sharks waited, they grew accustomed to these mysteries and ignored them, just as they ignored the miraculous throbbing stars. At midday the illusions merged into the sky and there the sun gazed down like an angry eye. Then, at the end of the afternoon, the mirage subsided and the horizon became level and blue and clipped as the sun declined."

Trying to describe this phenomena and how it fools human perception challenged other writers, as well.

The Americn poet Henry Wadsworth Longfellow, in a poem titled "Fata Morgana," described a similar illusory moment--

> As the weary traveler sees
> In desert or prairie vast,
> Blue lakes, overhung with trees
> That a pleasant shadow cast;
>
> Fair towns with turrets high,
> And shining roofs of gold,
> That vanish as he draws nigh,
> Like mists together rolled --

We trust our senses to provide us facts about the world, but then, we meet something as strange as Fata Morgana, and our senses fail us. They don't give us the information we need or expect. As a result, other judgements, such as time, are also skewed.

As we grow up, we learn to judge the duration of events. Estimating intervals of time is a skill we use daily; however, on the northern coast of Greenland, I have no idea how long I stood watching the mountains. I felt completely unable to sense or measure time. It may have been just a few minutes. It may have been much longer. My focus on them was absolute. I had no attention left for the Benedict Mountains at my back or for my teammates in our camp. I could only see the mountains rising above the sea ice.

Knowing they were not real did not diminish them. In fact, they became perhaps more enticing, like mountains of a dream, which is exactly what they were.

At some point, the mountains vanished as the vision had for the traveler in Longfellow's poem. Not knowing how long I had been away from camp, I decided I should return. I walked on the sea ice along the shore, the shredded ice again crunching under my boots.

I had had an advantage over the early explorers. I had read about Fata Morgana and understood the illusion. However, when I paused there and watched, it appeared so real. I understood why they had been confused when mountains seemed to rise in front of them.

I had seen other distortions in the mountains. Once while climbing Ben Nevis in Scotland, my climbing partner John Jancik and I had been shrouded in fog so heavy that we could not see the trail in front of us. Earlier climbers had built rock cairns six feet tall to keep climbers on the trail and away from the severe cliffs in such misty conditions. As we spied each cairn, our senses were so confused by the fog that we had trouble knowing if the cairn was ten feet away or fifty feet away. Each cairn seem to simply grow out of the fog and then dissolve as we walked past it.

I have seen blizzards in Montana that baffle the senses. Visions of distant buildings and trees move in and out of clarity, like waves of sight moving in the storm. The snowflakes absorb sound, so for example, the noise of a moving car sounds as if it is at a different angle.

Perhaps seeing things is more than just transferring light rays through the optic nerve to the brain. That image is then interpreted, sifted through the life, the experiences, the culture we bring to the process of understanding.

What if other truths in our lives have a touch of Fata Morgana in them?

I wondered about our other senses, what we hear and what we taste, and speculated on a form of Fata Morgana for them. What if the senses we rely on so deeply don't always present us with accurate information? If our senses are skewed, what chance, then, do we have of perceiving time with even a slice of accuracy?

If elements of our world are sometimes cloaked in illusion, we have the interesting task of sorting out what is distortion and what is reality. I hoped that most of our perceptions, like the mountains we climbed in northern Greenland, are real, solid and firm, but my brief encounter with the projected mountains of shattered sea ice, let me know that sometimes we have to be aware and question what we perceive.

Along that line of thinking then, what traditions, beliefs, institutions, and assumptions in our lives are mountains rising out of the sea ice?

I remembered times when I had heard a lesson from a professor, comments from a politician, or ideas in a book that confused me, sent my head spinning. The solution was to find someone else who experienced the same thing and compare understandings, reach a sort of middle ground on what was happening and what the meaning might be.

On the coast of Greenland, I did the same thing. I returned to our camp and asked if anyone had seen the same Fata Morgana moments earlier. Some had. They were as excited as I was, and I said something about the shining mountains on the horizon. One teammate stopped and looked at me. He hadn't seen mountains. He had seen the skyline of a crystalline city, buildings and skyscrapers of glistening glass.

I couldn't even trust my own illusion.

A Moment of Darkness in South Dakota

_____
_____

Chapter 2

The Stone Back Rub
Spring 1973

The opening to the crawlway seem small. I had watched Charlie bend down, enter headfirst, and squirm through it. His ankles flexed as he pushed with the toes of his boots. His hips rotated slightly, side to side, and I could hear his Levi's rub against the rock walls and floor. As he moved forward, less and less of his legs were visible. Finally his boots disappeared into the tunnel, and the scraping sounds were all that remained. A minute or two later, I heard his voice.

"OK. I'm in the room on the other side. Come on through."

We were deep in Jasper Cave in the Black Hills of western South Dakota. The narrow opening in front of me was called Ryan's Wriggle. I never knew Ryan, but he must have been pretty skinny. I had watched Charlie go through. He was two inches taller than me, and as a college swimmer, had broader shoulders than I did. If he went through there, I should be able to do it, I thought.

Down on my hands and knees, shining my flashlight into Ryan's Wriggle, those thoughts did not comfort me. It looked small. Tight. I had never thought of myself as claustrophobic, but something was happening inside.

I flattened onto my stomach. I put both arms in front of me, hands outstretched, as if I were diving into a lake. I held my flashlight in my left hand, and scooted forward into the entrance of the tunnel.

"It will be easier if you turn your head to one side," Charlie said. "That way you won't bump it on the roof."

It was reassuring to hear his voice, even though I was struggling with doubt.

I turned my face to the right, dropped my left cheek down to the floor, and quickly realized he was right. I pushed forward with my knees until my shoulders entered the tunnel. I pulled with my fingers and pushed with my toes, as I had seen Charlie do. It was slow progress, an inch or two at a time, but soon I was fully inside the crawlway. My chest was pressed against the floor of the tunnel. I could feel the sides lightly scrape against the outsides of my shoulder blades. The ceiling gave me a stone back rub.

My breathing was short and shallow. I wasn't sure if that was a fear response, or if I was unconsciously trying to keep my chest and ribs narrow. I continued to pull with my fingers and push with my toes. I tried a sort of walking motion with my chest with each pull and push. The pulling and pushing became a rhythm, and I relaxed a little.

"It sounds like you are getting closer," Charlie said. I didn't respond.

Ten feet does not seem very far until you are inside a rock tube. I know I only took a minute or two to get through Ryan's Wriggle, as Charlie had, but facing that challenge more than one hundred feet underground made each finger pull, each toe push transform into cave time. A tunnel like Ryan's Wriggle had taken thousands of years to form. A stalactite or a stalagmite dripped into place over millions of years. Against that patient framework, my belly slide was an Olympic luge run.

Charlie Gregalis was my roommate. We were freshmen at Chadron State College in Nebraska, an hour's drive south of the Black Hills. Charlie had gone to Jasper Cave before with a Sierra Club outing. He came back very excited about his experience and wanted others of us from the dorm to try it. We agreed, not knowing exactly what we were getting into.

"Take your oldest clothes," he said. "They will get torn on the parts where we have to crawl."

We sorted clothing, borrowed some helmets, and found enough flashlights and batteries.

When the weekend arrived, we loaded up a car and drove north. The Black Hills are beautiful, lakes surrounded by meadows and thick forests. Until we started reading and talking about caving, I did not realize what an extensive network of caves existed below the surface. It was a hidden world. There are signs advertising several commercial caves, but an abundance of smaller, out-of-the-way caves form a honeycomb throughout the region.

We drove to Custer, South Dakota, then headed west toward Newcastle, Wyoming. Charlie pulled us over at an obscure turnout blocked by a barbed-wire gate. We parked the car and hiked a mile to the cave entrance. At that time, it had a metal gate, like I would imagine in an Old West town jail. Charlie opened the gate, and I remember feeling that mixture of dread and anticipation that accompanies the first-timer on any venture that he knows will be a memorable experience, but has the potential to be dangerous as well.

Inside the gate, the opening to the cave was large. We could easily walk inside, so it seemed inviting. However, ten feet inside the door, I was on the seat of my pants, slowly sliding legs first into a black pit which appeared to have no bottom.

Caves breathe, and according to the outside barometric pressure, will breathe in or out. On this day, Jasper Cave breathed out. The wind blew tiny particles of dirt and sand into our faces. This same wind, funneled through the narrow passage, made it impossible to talk. Moving into the darkness was a strange transition. We had talked about it, but living it felt unsettling.

We climbed straight down a hole, appropriately named Wind Tunnel, which allowed us to use our hands and feet on both sides. It was easy to move downward. Many handholds and footholds protruded from the walls, as if we were inside a wide chimney. At the bottom, we entered a room where we stopped to wait for everyone to get down the chimney. The wind, which had been so powerful at the narrow entrance tunnel was nearly lost in the larger room.

Charlie led us through an opening into a side-sloping passage called Manganese Alley. As we moved farther along, we were continually descending deeper into the earth. We could often walk bent over, but frequently had to crawl through lower sections. At the end of Manganese Alley, the hallway opened into the Two-Dome Room. As the name suggests, the ceiling of the room formed two domes, like smaller versions of a capitol rotunda. The many rocks that had broken off the ceiling to form the domes littered the floor of the room. We sat on the rocks for a few minutes, talking and marveling at where we were and what we were doing.

"At the far end of the room is a passage that drops down and then takes us to a really fun climb called Prince Albert's Chimney," Charlie said. Charlie seemed relaxed and confident. Talking about the features of the cave convinced me he knew where we were going. I needed that. This whole process seemed alien to me.

I had been in a few commercial caves in the Black Hills. I had visited Wind Cave, Rushmore Cave, Diamond Crystal Cave, and others. I enjoyed visiting them, especially in summer when the cool air inside the cave felt refreshing. Caves stay the same temperature year round. Because they are underground, they are not affected by the surface weather patterns. The temperature of a cave is usually close to the average year-round temperature of the region where it is located, so Jasper Cave stayed in the mid-40s. That temperature provided pleasant surroundings for all the walking, climbing, and crawling we were doing.

Other than temperature, being in a commercial cave was a very different experience. The walkways are always large enough to stand up. If they weren't high enough naturally, they are often drilled or otherwise enlarged to accommodate people and prevent tourists from banging their heads on overhanging rock. The walkways are often modified. If they are not flat initially, they are usually paved or covered in wooden or metal paths. Any incline or decline is apt to feature steps and handrails. Electric lights flood those caves in artificial daylight and spotlights frequently highlight special stalagmites, stalactites, as well as ribbons, flows, popcorn, or other intricate formations.

Commercial caves make it safe and easy for anyone to admire the underground world. I had loved visiting them, but they are far different from what we were experiencing on our rag-tag spelunking trip into Jasper Cave.

We moved down into that passage and found easy going. It was wider, taller, and let us walk comfortably. We directed our flashlights around the walls of the cave, looking for any interesting formations, watching for smaller side passages or rooms.

Soon a wall stopped our progress. Facing that wall, we could see a steep ramp leading upward and to our left. Lower and to the right was a narrow passage.

"This goes up into Prince Albert's Chimney," Charlie said, pointing his flashlight toward the ramp and following it upward. Then, shining his flashlight lower, he said, "Take a look at this narrow opening and remember it. I'll tell you more about it later."

Since we entered the cave, we had been descending most of the time. At first, in Wind Tunnel, it had been straight down. Then through Manganese Alley, the Two-Dome Room, and the passageway beyond that, it had been a more gradual descent with a few spots of steeper drop. At the ramp, we started up. Prince Albert's Chimney, as Charlie had said, was fun climbing. It was not vertical, but nearly so. Steep with plenty of handholds and footholds on all sides. We climbed fifty feet to a small, flat spot, then immediately turned and headed down. That chimney was narrow, tighter than Prince Albert's Chimney, but just as steep. It was named The Bat Trap, and we downclimbed thirty-five or forty feet into a small room with another passage out the far side. Some mixed walking, stooping, and crawling led us to The Registry Room. A hole in the floor of that room let us drop down a tunnel and enter a room whose obvious shape gave it the name The T-Room.

We had reached the end of Jasper Cave. We had plenty of room for all of us to sit down, rest, and eat lunch. I could see the faces of my friends. There were a lot of smiles. Everyone was excited, but not like fans at a football game. We weren't cheering, or jumping up and down. It was a subtle excitement. A deep sense of awe.

"Think about where we are," Kevin said. "We've come down

quite a ways in the dark. There are tons of rock over our heads. It's a little mind-boggling."

While we were eating, we decided to turn off the flashlights. I had seen guides do this in the commercial caves, and it was always interesting to experience total darkness; however, the visitors know the guide, with the flip of a switch, could blanket the entire cave with vital light. For us, no switch existed. Sitting there with friends, knowing we had reached this point under our own power, knowing we were responsible for getting ourselves back out, was a powerful moment for our group.

From the T-Room, we reversed our path, began the steady trek upward through The Registry Room, up the short tunnel into the room below The Bat Trap. Crawling through that tunnel, I noticed one thing which I think most people who enter a cave experience. The route looked different going backwards. The rock formations, the bumps in the walls, the undulations in the floor all appeared completely new. On hikes Charlie and I had taken in the national forest, I had seen how sharp his memory was. He could notice trees and rocks that marked our way. Now, deep underground, his photographic memory for routes was even more valuable.

When we reached the room below The Bat Trap, Charlie paused. He explained that the cave split. We could climb up The Bat Trap and down Prince Albert's Chimney on the other side, or we could take a shorter route back, but it involved the tight crawlway called Ryan's Wriggle. We decided to try the shortcut.

Being underground in the dark affects human senses. My eyes were tired. Staring into the darkness, trying to follow the beam of the flashlight was draining. Sounds seemed muffled, yet at the same time distinct. My fingers and palms felt numb, raw from holding tightly onto rough rocks. My elbows and knees were scratched. The air smelled musty.

One big difference I felt was a loss of direction. When walking or driving, I generally felt I had a good sense of where north was. I could keep track of where I was and orient myself on a map quickly. Underground, in the depths of Jasper Cave, I was clueless. We had climbed up and down, turned left and right, walked and crawled, and I had no idea which direction we were moving. In one way it didn't matter. We could only go where the cave allowed us to go. We weren't walking through a forest, but were following a route that was defined. Still, I did not like the unaccustomed disorientation.

I pulled with my fingers and pushed with my toes. Many of the parts of the cave had been a challenge, but nothing came close to the confines of Ryan's Wriggle. At last my outstretched hands felt an edge. I tilted my head back the little I could, and saw a small glow from Charlie's light. I pulled on the edge and slid my head into the passage where we had turned to go up Prince Albert's Chimney on our way in.

Exhilaration.

Ryan's Wriggle had been a test, a strenuous physical problem, yes, but a more difficult mental move. Overcoming both at once in a ten-foot space filled me with joy. What a strange sport where success is the ability to cram one's body through such a small place.

I smiled at Charlie. We stood together and listened as the others pulled, pushed, grunted, their way through Ryan's Wriggle. Finally, with all of us past that crux, we walked back through The Two Dome Room and into Manganese Alley. Perhaps it was because we were tired, or I was distracted by the overwhelming experience of Ryan's Wriggle, but returning through the sloping slabs in Manganese Alley was much more difficult. Bending down to pass through openings, I hooked a rock overhead and ripped the back of my shirt. Twice I tore my jeans on the sharp stones of the floor and walls. Manganese Alley seemed intent on charging a price before letting us leave Jasper Cave.

At the end of Manganese Alley, we were almost directly under the entrance to the cave. When we had entered the cave, the transition from light to dark, from horizontal to vertical shocked us. The cave breathing, blowing sand up into our faces, had annoyed us, but now, after the climbs and crawls and wriggles, going up The Wind Tunnel was a breeze, so to speak. When we reached the top of Wind Tunnel, we got the first hints of daylight. We moved quickly onto the flat walkway, and pushed through the iron gate into full daylight.

It was like awakening. After the darkness and the restricted movement inside the cave, the sunshine and open space felt like freedom. Regaining the light expanded the world. We smelled the pine trees and breathed the warm, fresh air. We laughed.

We had left a backpack near the entrance. Some clean clothes. Extra food. Water. We changed shirts and examined scratched elbows and knees. We ate and drank. We laughed even more. Kevin reached in the pocket of the pack and pulled out a watch. We had been inside Jasper Cave for four hours. The darkness and twisting tunnels had not only removed my sense of direction, but had totally distorted time. If he had said eight hours or twelve hours, I would have easily believed him. The cave had challenged us physically, mentally, emotionally, and returning to daylight was a reorientation to the world.

As we walked to the car, I paused and looked back at the iron gate. Somewhere beyond that gate, deep beneath the forest, places like Prince Albert's Chimney and Ryan's Wriggle existed in silent blackness.

A Moment of Grandeur in the Crazy Mountains

———————
————

Chapter 3

Suspended in Dark Space
August 4, 1993

After twelve hours of climbing sharp mountain ridges, we were tired and out of water. We had hoped to cross one more mountain and sleep on the saddle beyond it, but we were running out of daylight, and the rugged terrain was far too difficult to climb in the dark. The slope we were on was precipitous, dropping over a thousand feet to the valley below. Angry clouds were building to the west. We had climbed ourselves into a difficult situation.

We arrived at a small snowfield, the first possible water source we had seen in hours. Joe Sears, a research chemist at Montana State University in Bozeman at that time, dropped his backpack on the rocks, removed his stove, and set it up to melt snow for water. It was clear that by the time we had enough water to get through the night, it would be dark. We would have to spend the night; however, there were no places flat enough for two people to sleep.

I moved away from the snowfield and the ridge leading up the mountain and found an area of loose rocks that I could easily move. I pieced together two small ledges, fitting rocks together like jig-saw puzzles, trying to make the ledges as flat as possible. It seemed to take longer than I wanted, but by the time Joe walked over with bottles of water, I had two ledges, each two feet wide and five feet long. The sun had dropped behind the peaks to the west, so these ledges, insignificant as they were, would have to work for the night.

"At that point, I was not too concerned about us," Joe later said. "If we could get water and have a good dinner, I expected we would be OK. The weather wasn't too bad, but it started changing when it got dark. I had a good sleeping bag and bivy sack and thought we would be fine."

Using the last minutes of daylight, we ate dinner, drank plenty of water, and sorted our packs and sleeping bags on the primitive ledges. Joe wondered if we would be able to sleep on the ledges without rolling off. Good question.

We were on Day 3 of an attempt to traverse the Crazy Mountains in central Montana. We had never heard of anyone climbing so many of these mountains in one trip. Few people have ever even heard of the Crazy Mountains, and compared to Yellowstone National Park, Grand Teton National Park, or Glacier National Park, they are seldom visited - just the place for us. The Crazy Mountains are north of Big Timber, Montana, and Interstate 90. Most people driving

Joe Sears pours meltwater into his bottle as he prepares to spend a night on the small ledges overlooking a thousand-foot drop into the valley. The heavy rain began less than an hour after this photo was taken. Photo by Steve Gardiner

the Interstate give the Crazies a quick glance and never think of them again. I had done the same, but now that we were deep in the middle of the range, my respect for these mountains had changed dramatically.

The Crazy Mountains are a north-south range, so we got the idea to leave a car at the south end, drive to the north end, and walk the entire length of the range by connecting as many summits as possible. Sitting on the floor in Joe's living room in Bozeman and using a dot-to-dot method on a map, we had seen a logical route through the range. We were hooked on the idea.

As we were researching the trip, we found a note about the Crazy Mountains in a book called the *Climbers Guide to Montana*. Author Pat Caffrey wrote, "The Crazies are the most primitive, forbidding mountains in the state. The ridges, bare bones of God's green earth, are obviously on poor terms with most forms of plant life. The absence of an even half-hearted mountain serenity on such a grand scale is awesome, as the range makes not even a pretense of hospitality. Ascents are nothing harder than scrambles, but these are hard scrambles. The peaks are remote, the routes long, and the footing is, though variable, never firm."

Joe and I understood that stark description.

Because we knew we would be sleeping on rocky ground, and because we wanted to save weight, we had not brought a tent on this trip. Instead, we had two bivy sacks, narrow fabric bags that slip over a sleeping bag to provide, in theory, protection from the elements. Bivy sacks serve a useful purpose, but have the disadvantage that it is not possible to sit up or get dressed inside it as would be possible with a tent. Given our perch on the small ledges, we would not have been able to pitch a tent, even if we had had one.

The clouds grew thicker. Darkness settled on us. Inside of our sleeping bags, we each tried to find the least damaging position to rest on the rocks. We had trained well for the trip, but we had not practiced sleeping on small, rocky ledges overlooking a black abyss. This was a new experience.

I thought back on the previous two days. On Day 1, we left Joe's car at the south end of the range and drove my car to the north end. From there, we hiked four hours, getting lost several times on trails that seemed well-used but soon faded to nothing. We walked through heavy forest, crossed streams, found trails and lost them using Sunlight Peak as our beacon when we could see it through the trees. We camped on a grassy saddle beneath Sunlight Peak. That put us in fine shape to begin climbing the next morning.

Early on Day 2, we climbed Sunlight Peak. From the top, we saw most of the Crazy Mountains spread out before us and connected the peaks with our eyes as we had earlier in our minds and on the map. We set off across a long string of unnamed peaks that formed the ragged spine of the range. We spent twelve hours that day climbing up the north ridge and down the south ridge of ten mountains. It had been straightforward climbing, enjoyable, energetic. We camped on a narrow pass that night, feeling excitement for the next day and for the remainder of the trip.

The next morning, Day 3, we spotted a deep notch, at least 150 vertical feet on each side and soon realized that it was right on the route we had chosen. The sheer notch would have required rappelling and roped climbing to cross it. We were not expecting major technical difficulties, so we had no ropes with us. That forced us to drop 600-700 feet down into the valley to scramble around the notch. Beyond the next peak was a similar notch followed by a nasty, serrated ridge. Twice more we had to drop low to pass these problems. This up and down work made our progress slow.

"We did not expect the serious nature of the rugged interior peaks," Joe recalled. "It was totally surprising, and yet we loved it. We appreciated the beauty and severe nature of those mountains. We had to drop down a long ways to move around those obstacles that day. It was a big challenge to work our way through that crux central area of the range."

Because of the difficult nature of the terrain, we only climbed three mountains on the third day. We had hoped to climb and descend a fourth and sleep on what looked like, on the map, a suitable saddle, however, that was when the lack of water, increasing clouds, and oncoming darkness convinced us to stop, melt snow, and build the two small ledges.

"We intended to hike full days throughout the trip, and that was what we were doing," Joe said, "but on our way up the fourth peak (on Day 3), we realized that we were going to run out of time."

Running out of time had been an ongoing joke. When we were thirty, we landed on the idea that "We've only got five good years left." It seemed like many athletes ended their careers about thirty-five, so we started talking about how to use the time we had left to finish the best climbs we could.

A year later, the joke evolved to "We only have four good years left." It inspired more discussions of what peaks we should climb. With each passing year, the number dropped and our plans continued.

Inevitably, we reached thirty-five and showed no tendency to stop or even slow down. We kidded ourselves that we were climbing on extended time, past our prime, but still going. We made more plans, climbed more mountains, and our joke about "good years left" disappeared.

By ten p.m., the clouds we had seen building over the mountains in the west brought rain. It started with a light patter, but soon increased. I could hear the crinkle of Joe's bivy sack as he rolled over, trying to get the rain out of his face and stay dry. The rain came harder. Then it was pouring. All we could do was curl up on our small ledges.

I could feel the night rain leak through the covering of my sleeping bag and form puddles beneath my shoulder and hip. I shivered and pulled my knees up closer to my chest trying to save as much warmth as possible. The rocks all around us were wet, dangerously slippery. I thought about the lake and snowfield over a thousand feet below my narrow ledge. We could only hope the rain stopped soon.

The Crazy Mountains are as spectacular as any mountains I've seen, and the isolation of the central peaks equals an Alaskan experience. But strangely enough, the range is not part of any park, refuge, or wilderness area. The entire range and surrounding region is National Forest land and as such, has remained very untouched and unknown. We were certainly aware of that sense of remoteness as we lay on the ledges, pounded by rain.

"I didn't expect such a drenching downpour," Joe said. "I remember rolling over and realizing that my bivy sack was leaking and collecting water inside. My sleeping bag was a lightweight down bag, and it was soaked, so it was worthless. I thought, 'This is more serious now.'"

I remember wondering about hypothermia. How long could we lay on the rocky ledges in heavy rain before our core body temperatures dropped to dangerous levels?

A year earlier, Joe and I had had an experience with hypothermia in the Beartooth Mountains of Montana. We had hiked up the Lake Fork Trail and branched off on a slight trail to Black Canyon Lake. We camped near the edge of the morainal dam that formed the lake. During the night, five mountain goats had wandered next to our tent, munching on the soft grass. It was a beautiful night, so we had left the tent door open. We could lie in our sleeping bags and watch the goats eating.

The next morning, we set out with rock climbing gear to a vertical granite wall about five hundred feet tall. Perhaps someone else had climbed it, but I had never heard about anyone who had. We were fascinated by it.

We selected a series of ledges and cracks and started climbing up them. We hoped to climb the steep face to a point where it connected with a sloping southwest ridge. We would then be able to use the ridge for our descent. We took turns leading, using a rope for protection and setting secure anchors in the cracks. We climbed up four rope lengths, and I was setting an anchor when a swift-moving cloud system moved in. Within minutes we were drenched in freezing rain.

I finished setting the anchor, but instead of using it to protect Joe as he climbed up, I would be using it to rappel off. With the rain, we could not attempt to meet the ridge and descend it. I slid down the rope to Joe. As I was rappelling, I looked down at him. The crack system we had used for the anchor was recessed a few inches into the face of the rock. That recess was a perfect channel for the freezing rain pelting us. Water hit the face of the rock wall and funneled straight down into Joe's chest. Because he was attached to the climbing anchor, Joe could not move out of the way of the icy river.

We moved as quickly as we could while still maintaining safety. We set two more anchors and rappelled to the ground. Because we needed to thread our rope through each anchor and pull it down for the next rappel, we would lose all the equipment we put in the anchors. Neither of us were concerned about that loss. We were more concerned about body temperature. We were both shivering, even in the middle of the afternoon.

By the time we reached the ground, the freezing rain had stopped. The rocks were dripping, and we were soaked. We staggered half a mile back to our tent, set up the stove, and spent the next two hours drinking hot tea, snuggled inside our sleeping bags. The climbing had been exhilarating, but the descent in the icy rain had drained us of all energy. We drank hot tea until we stopped shaking, then were ready to sleep at six p.m.

That night on our ledges in the Crazy Mountains, "It rained very hard from about ten until one in the morning," Joe explained. "By then, everything we had was soaking wet. My backpack was wet. All of our food was wet, and much of it was ruined. All of our extra clothing was wet."

When the rain quit, we examined our situation. The night wasn't dark, it was black. The rocks were far too wet for us to move around. Descent in the night was out of the question. We would have to wait for the dawn and the warmth that sunlight and movement would bring.

Joe had an idea. "My bivy sack was a homemade version, and it was not working at all. I grabbed my knife and cut it open, because I thought it would be big enough for both of us to get under it. We draped it across our backs and shoulders and sat side by side. We put the stove between us and were careful to keep our legs away from the flames."

We heated a pot of water and drank it. The hot water revived us, although we knew it would be several hours before we could move or do anything about the situation we were in. We decided that every hour we would heat a pot of water and drink. After three hours of heavy rain, we were both wet and cold. We sat together on the ledge. We talked little and slept not at all.

An hour later, we started the stove and heated another pot of water. We were too cold and tired to try to rummage through the sack of food, damaged by the downpour, to find tea bags or hot chocolate, so we decided we would just drink the hot water. It was the heat and hydration we needed, so though not tasty, it would serve its purpose.

At three a.m., we heated another pot of water. We were still shivering. The benefit of the hot water may have been more psychological than physical. At least starting the stove and waiting for the water to boil was a break from the monotony of sitting on the cold ledge staring into the night.

It had become obvious that the rainstorm had been a major event in this trip. I don't remember which one of us asked the question or made the suggestion, but we talked several minutes about our immediate future. We had made a careful and exciting plan of traversing the entire range of the Crazy Mountains by going from summit to summit. We had already crossed thirteen mountains and had a few more ahead of us, but with wet clothing, damaged food, and tired bodies, we needed to reexamine our plan. This was not an easy discussion, because Joe and I are both people who have a habit of finishing projects. However, at this point, it seemed to both of us that getting out safely was more important than achieving our ultimate goal. It was too dark to pull out the map and try to make any serious decisions, but from memory, we constructed a simple plan that could be advanced when we had daylight and some warmth from the sun.

Our new plan would be to wait for sunrise and then descend

from this point to the lake below. We knew there was a trail that would lead to our car at the southern end of the range, but we did not know what obstacles might lie between us and that trail. At this point, that much planning would have to suffice. We could work out the details later.

"At about four a.m., we decided to get up and move around," Joe said. "We wanted to do some jumping jacks and get warmed up, but we made a mistake by doing that. We quickly froze."

We had only removed the tarp for a brief time, but we were immediately chilled. We fired the stove and again drank a pot of hot water. We were shivering and wishing for sunrise.

We sat on the ledge, huddled together, and looked out over the plains. In the distance we could see the lights from the town of Livingston and imagined the people there, sitting in their homes, warm and comfortable.

Like students waiting for the school bell to ring, we were restless, needing to move, but the night, the cold, and the cliff held us in place.

Remembering being on the ledge at five a.m., Joe said, "We did not think we were in danger, even though we were very cold and stiff. The hardest thing was just sitting there, being so cold and wet. We never thought we would freeze or get injured, but we did know we would have to be careful. It was a long drop below. The rocks around us were wet and slick. Ice was every place."

We were suspended in dark space.

Chapter 4

Fists and Thumbs
June 10, 1976

Joe and I had been roommates my senior year at Chadron State College in western Nebraska. It's not uncommon for college roommates to have fights. Disagreements over when the lights go out or where dirty clothes should land often cause problems, but when Joe and I were roommates, we fought almost daily with punches and kicks. We were both training hard to earn our black belts in Taekwondo, preparing to demonstrate our skills in front of a panel of seven Korean masters. We pushed each other to train harder, to perfect the kicks and punches we would need to succeed in the martial arts. We worked on our patterns, repeating them until every small move was memorized, engrained in our muscles. We learned to break boards and free fight. Those sparring matches also helped us develop a deep sense of respect for each other which carried over when we started rock climbing and mountaineering together.

As roommates, one of our first adventures together had been in 1976, the year of the American Bicentennial. We decided that since neither of us had been to the East Coast, it was our duty, as young Americans, to go see some of the historical sites of our nation. One problem. No money. We were poor college students..

We decided to hitchhike to New York, Boston, and Washington, DC. We lucked out by helping two other students drive east. After that, we caught other rides, and in less than two days, we were in upstate New York. We spent a couple of days with a friend, then we split up. Joe went to Albany to see a friend, and I went to Connecticut to see a group of friends. Two days later, we talked on the phone and realized that the main highway south from Albany, and the main highway going west out of Connecticut crossed near Newburgh, New York. We were young and optimistic, so we set a time and agreed to meet at the bridge where the two highways intersected.

The next day I thumbed a quick ride that took me straight to the bridge. I got out and looked around. No Joe. I waited a few minutes, but I could see another bridge a quarter of a mile away. I decided to walk to that bridge, just in case he was waiting there. That was a mistake. I had been walking on the edge of the road for a hundred yards when a New York State Trooper pulled over. He questioned me and gave me the tongue-lashing I deserved. "You are from Nebraska? And you are trying to meet your friend at a bridge on the turnpike? Could you be more stupid?" At that point I couldn't argue with him.

The trooper directed me to return to the bridge, sit under it, and if I found Joe, I was to disappear and never be seen on the turnpike again. I walked back to the bridge and sat down. Less than five minutes later, the trooper pulled up and stopped in front of me. Sitting in the back seat of the car was Joe. Imagine Joe's surprise when the trooper had pulled up beside him on the highway, rolled down his window, and asked, "Are you from Nebraska?"

I walked to the patrol car. "Get in," he said. We drove a few miles down the road and exited at a state patrol office. "I need to do some work inside," he said. "I assume you two will be sitting here when I return."

Trying to sleep on the small rock ledges in the Crazy Mountains was uncomfortable, but nothing like the eternity we spent sitting in the patrol car waiting for the trooper to come back and let us go.

We went on to Concord, Massachusetts. We wanted to see the Minuteman Monument and other Revolutionary War sites. As an English major, I thought it would be a good cultural experience for Joe, a science major, to visit Walden Pond and pay his respects to Henry David Thoreau, one of my favorite authors.

After spending the day touring historical sites, we ate dinner in a small cafe on the main street of Concord. It was getting late, and we were not sure what we were going to do for the night.

When we walked out of the cafe, a young man stopped his car and asked, "Are you hitchhiking?" We gave him a brief account, and he asked where we wanted to go. We told him Walden Pond, and he said he would take us. We drove out of Concord, and he dropped us off near Walden Pond. He said if we moved farther into the trees, we could camp, because it was not allowed right at the Pond. It was a highlight for me.

In Boston, we saw Boston Common, Harvard Yard, and a host of other sites, then headed south to Washington, DC. We had good luck finding rides no matter where we wanted to go. At that time, it was still safe to hitchhike, and we looked at those rides as chances to meet new people, to hear their stories, and to share our own. Getting the free rides helped, because we were traveling on a zero budget.

A friend had told us that in Washington, DC, we should stop by the dorms at Georgetown University, and we could probably find a place to stay for the night. It was raining as we walked to Georgetown, so when we arrived, we were drenched. The night attendant at the desk said there was no way we could stay in the dorm, but if we wanted, we could sleep on the floor in the laundry room. The price was right, so we went to the laundry room. A breeze was blowing in a broken window, chilling us in our wet clothing. It was an uncomfortable night, and the attendant woke us too early. His shift was over, so we had to leave. We spent the day walking all over Washington, and by early afternoon, our rough night caught up with us. We ended up taking a nap on the park benches in front of the Jefferson Memorial.

By late afternoon, it was raining again. We decided hitchhiking in the rain would be too difficult. The novelty of standing on the side of the road, waiting for a ride, was wearing off. We voted to get a Greyhound bus ticket to start us west to Nebraska. On the way to the bus station, the rain was the hardest we had seen. We were soaked as we stood in line to buy tickets. Just as the clerk handed us our tickets, the driver called for passengers to board the bus. We took turns in the restroom on the bus, changing into the last dry clothing we had.

Heading home, we decided to count our money. By hitchhiking, camping out, staying with friends, and watching our budget, we had spent $120 each for a two-week vacation. We had learned how to be poor college students.

While changing clothes, we had both noticed how wrinkled our hands and feet were from two days of walking in the rain and sleeping in the laundry room. We laughed. We did not know then that the wrinkled hands and feet foreshadowed a wet night we would spend on a perch in the Crazy Mountains in Montana seventeen years later.

Chapter 5

A Trip Takes Us
August 5, 1993

I always love the dawn, but how can I explain the joy we felt when we finally got early morning light on our ledges? That light brought us hope.

Joe explained one problem. "In the morning we tried to pack our gear in our backpacks. Everything weighed twice as much because of all the water we were carrying. At six a.m., the sun came up, and we made our break. We went down as quickly as was safely possible on wet rocks after a night of no sleep. It was difficult to get our legs to support us. We were wobbly, weak, not focused like we usually are when climbing."

We descended the thousand feet to the lake. It was hard to move on wet rocks with cold muscles, but by the time we reached the valley floor, we were in direct sunlight. We pulled wet clothes and sleeping bags out of our packs, wringing the water from each item. We spread wet clothing over the rocks and poured water out of every bag and container we owned.

We were off the steep rocks and on level ground.

"It was not a trivial descent by any means," Joe noted. "The rocks were coated in ice, and we moved very slowly, not wanting to sprain or break an ankle so far removed from any source of help. We knew we had to keep moving and that it would be a long day. It would be difficult walking with heavy packs. We also knew we could not spend another night out. We were too tired, too cold and had very little food left to eat."

Our clothing and sleeping bags were still wet, but at least we had drained the excess water. We were cold and stiff, so we wanted to keep moving. We found a faint trail that led to a lake. From our view above on the day before, we were pretty sure we wanted to head in the direction of a snowy pass ahead of us. If we were right, on the other side of the pass, we would find a trail which would eventually lead us south out of the mountains.

We walked down one valley, turned to the east to go up a second valley as we searched for a pass that would take us to Rock Lake. We hoped to locate the trail that would lead us to our car, but first, we needed to rest and eat some breakfast. About eight o'clock, we dropped our backpacks to the ground and set up the stove to heat water for oatmeal and tea.

We had a long way to go. It would be hours of walking on weak legs, but we simply had to reach our car at the southern end of the range.

The tea and oatmeal were excellent. While we ate, we spread clothing and sleeping bags on rocks in the sun, hoping to get some drying effect. We were still cold inside, so the warmth of the sun was a relief.

I looked at the piles of wet gear all around us and remembered a friend who used to say, "I don't understand why my pack is so heavy. All I have is one hundred pounds of lightweight gear." All we had was wet gear.

During our rest break, we could look up and see several more mountains. The valley detour would cost us a few of the last summits we had intended to climb, but nature had given us no choice. It would not be a success according to our original plan, but we would still traverse the entire range and climb thirteen mountains in the process. It would be a different version of success.

We packed our backpacks again, and set out toward the south.

About ten a.m., the trail led us onto a large boulder field. Boulder-hopping is another skill that backpackers and mountain climbers must learn to move easily through rugged terrain. It's not hard, but it requires care, because the boulders can move. I've noticed that after years of walking over rocks, it was as if my feet knew where to go. The sounds of moving rocks seemed to alert them, and they responded, landing in solid places and keeping me in balance.

Usually.

I did take one slip and scraped my shin just above the top of my hiking boot.

Because the trail ended when we entered the boulder field, we tried to follow the contour of the hill, stay high and circle the slope. This, we hoped, would save us energy and time, and would also allow us to look down, in case we eventually picked up another section of trail and could return to easier walking.

After an hour of boulder-hopping, we walked near a small stream. It led to a lake where we could see the route to the snowy pass. We were deep in the heart of the Crazy Mountain range. We had views of a rugged cirque featuring a deep granite notch. The peaks rose high overhead.

"The Crazy Mountains are so remote and vast," Joe said. "If you see the Crazies from Interstate 90, they look small, but when you are in the middle, they are a big range with spectacular peaks."

These mountains had punished us, but we could still appreciate their beauty. We watched them as we proceeded, moving toward the snowy pass.

We climbed the steep pass, which in our tired state took us much longer than we expected. At the top of the pass, we were in heavy clouds and fog. After our night on the cold, wet ledges, we were not in the mood for more rain, and the thought of hiking in rain now seemed like torture. From the pass, we could get a view of Rock Lake below us. That was hopeful. It was noon. The sun had warmed the snowfield, so there was a layer of mushy snow two or three inches deep over the harder snow beneath. Conditions like that make it easy to slide on the snow using either a skating motion or a downhill skiing technique with boots. This section of snow was steep enough that boot skiing worked perfectly, and we slid down the slope, stopping to walk when we got close to the rocks near the bottom.

After an hour, we reached the base of the snowfield and walked toward the valley floor. We felt much more relaxed there. The difficulty of the icy, morning descent and the crossing of the snowy pass were behind us. We had arrived in the valley we needed, and we located the trail. It was much fainter than we expected. We got lost several times before the trail became solid and gave us a strong sense of moving toward Joe's car.

The trail led us to Rock Lake where we planned to take a break. It was two o'clock. It had been eight hours since we left our rocky ledges and six hours since our breakfast. The energy from the oatmeal was long gone. We set up the stove to boil water for Ramen noodles. As I listened to the hum of the stove and watched the first whisps of steam coming out of the pot, I could remember the many times Joe and I had camped together in dozens of mountain ranges. We had arrived at campsites tired and hungry, a combination that leads hikers to become more efficient in how they set up camp. We had learned to split the work with one of us setting up the stove, heating water, and making two cups of noodles. The other would set up the tent, spread out the sleeping bags, and organize the equipment and clothing inside. We would both put on dry socks and shirts and within minutes, we would be resting with a cup of hot noodles in front of our home for the night. It was always amazing how quickly this bit of organization and a dime's worth of noodles could completely change our attitudes.

After the noodles were hot, Joe handed me my thermal cup, filled to the brim. When we had been on our way to an expedition on the Harding Icefield in Alaska, Joe had stopped by a 7-11 store. In 1987, thermal coffee cups were a brand new idea. We had never seen them, but that morning, Joe bought two of them on his way to the airport. He gave one to me. We had used them during our two weeks on the Icefield and loved them. They were a perfect addition to our camping tools. When we left the Icefield and went sea kayaking, we were sitting near a campfire on a beach in Kachemack Bay, relaxing after dinner. The fire was cracking, and one snap launched a burning coal into the air. Joe had set his cup on the sand, and the burning coal landed squarely inside his cup, instantly burning a hole in the bottom of it. It is a bit ironic that Joe bought the cups, and his was

After thirty hours without sleep, Joe Sears reaches the bottom of the snowy pass he had to cross in search of the trail leading south out of the Crazy Mountains in Montana. Photo by Steve Gardiner

destroyed on the first trip. Mine was twenty-eight years old, and had fed me well on scores of trips covering hundreds of miles of hiking and climbing.

We sat in the sun at Rock Lake and enjoyed a moment of peace. The noodles worked their magic. The food and water improved our strength and attitudes, but too soon, it was time to hike again. We still had a long way to go, and it was well into the afternoon.

We resumed our walk, struggling under the weight of backpacks still full of wet clothes and equipment. The trail was good, for the most part, and we followed it for several miles through thick forest, across vast blooming meadows, and into knee-deep ice water streams.

Throughout the middle of the afternoon, we lost the trail a couple of times. I am not sure if the trail disappeared, or if it was our own mental and physical tiredness that caused us to lose concentration. When we misplaced the trail, we would stop, look around, and get back on track. At least now that we were in the valley, the general tendency of the trail was downhill. That was a good thing.

"The next passage in my journey is a love affair. I am in love with Montana," wrote John Steinbeck in his classic book *Travels with Charley: In Search of America*. "For other states I have admiration, respect, recognition, even some affection, but with Montana it is love."

Steinbeck, at the age of fifty-eight, set out with his dog Charley in a pickup with a camper built on the back. He named the truck Rocinante after Don Quixote's horse. Steinbeck intended to drive around America for several months to "rediscover this monster land." His work as a writer had taken him to many parts of the world, but he felt the need to reconnect with the land and people of America.

Of course, my favorite part of the book is his description of his time in Montana. He wrote, "It seems to me that Montana is a great splash of grandeur. The scale is huge but not overpowering. The land is rich with grass and color, and the mountains are the kind I would create if mountains were ever put on my agenda."

The desire to travel and see the world led him on many journeys. Each journey has its own personality, its own power over our lives, and he noted that "we do not take a trip; a trip takes us."

Joe and I were learning that lesson in the Crazy Mountains.

Chapter 6

Canoeing and Climbing
Summary, 1977

During the summer of 1977, Joe and I got jobs as counselors at a wilderness camp at the end of the Gunflint Trail in northern Minnesota. At that time, we had both done a little bit of hiking, backpacking, and canoeing, but we were still very much beginners in the outdoor sports world. In our jobs as camp counselors, we would be taking groups of boys, ages eight to fifteen, on trips into the Boundary Waters Canoe Area in Minnesota and Quetico Provincial Park across the border in Canada. With that in mind, we spent several days before the boys arrived, learning how to sail, canoe, and rock climb. Joe and I had had no experience at all with rock climbing, and we were immediately fascinated with it. Most of the summer would be spent canoeing the magnificent lakes of the region, with sailing and rock climbing as added adventures.

When the boys arrived, mostly from larger cities like Minneapolis and St. Paul, they were frightened. Many had never been outside of the city, and to find themselves in a place as remote as the end of the Gunflint Trail bothered them. They did not realize that it was going to get much more remote than that.

At that time, the Boundary Waters Canoe Area and Quetico Provincial Park were popular, but nothing like today. We often paddled all day without seeing other people. We did not need permits or reservations to go anywhere in either park. We did not need passports or any other paperwork to go up the Seagull River and into Canada. We just stopped at the customs office island, let them know where we were going and for how long, and we were on our way. We could camp at any lake and often had the privilege of looking over several campsites and picking out the best one. We simply looked at maps, chose interesting destinations, packed our food and equipment, and set out for several days at a time.

One of the first canoe trips we took was a route called the Man Chain. This circuit consists of a dozen lakes and gets its name from some of the lakes, including That Man Lake, No Man Lake, This Man Lake, and Other Man Lake. That trip took us four or five days, and gave a chance to teach the boys how to paddle and steer the canoe, how to pack the food and equipment in the backpacks, how to carry the canoe and packs on the portages between lakes, and how to read the maps and interpret where we were on a lake.

When the boys had arrived, their conversations often concerned the television shows they were missing or the food they wanted to eat. Many of them hated the freeze-dried meals we cooked on camp stoves each evening. The Man Chain changed the boys. They quickly saw how beautiful the lakes were, learned to appreciate the evening call of a loon on the lake, and enjoyed the constant motion that the canoe trips offered. It was an adventure every day, and they took on the challenges of paddling and helping with camp chores. This, I expect, is what their parents wanted when they sent the boys to a summer wilderness camp.

We paddled throughout most of each day. We never rushed or pushed the boys too hard, but kept moving, talking about what we saw and making sure everyone got a chance to hold the maps and guide the group of canoes across a lake, past the islands, and to the next portage.

As our summer in the Boundary Waters Canoe Area and Quetico Provincial Park was coming to an end, we decided we needed one special trip to finish off the summer. The main cabin at our camp had piles of maps, and we pulled out several and started a search. We found one loop of lakes that would take us through Quetico Provincial Park and out the east side into Canadian wilderness to a lake named Greenwood. There were no marks on the maps in that area, and a quick search through the trip reports filed by other counselors revealed nothing. We asked around. Even the counselors who had been there a few summers could remember no one going into that area. We decided to go.

There was a bulletin board in the dining room where counselors posted opportunities for the campers. These notes usually explained how long the trip would last, how difficult it would be, and what lakes, rivers, or other features would be involved. A typical trip from camp lasted four or five days, followed by a couple of days in camp, then another trip. Most of the trips were based on canoeing, but some counselors would post trips to take our sailboat up onto Saganaga Lake, straddling the U.S./Canadian border, the deepest and largest lake in the Boundary Waters. Other counselors would post day or overnight trips to nearby cliffs for rock climbing. Usually Joe and I would take a four-day trip, then go out for a day trip to go climbing, then plan another longer canoe trip. The mix made for a lot of fun and allowed us to work with a variety of the campers.

The season-finale trip to Greenwood Lake would be the most difficult of the summer. We estimated it would take nine days and include a long series of lakes and portages. It would be a challenge, but we found enough boys who were interested, and we set out.

The morning we left was drizzling. We were slow getting going, but that turned out to be a good thing. By the time we paddled the Seagull River to Saganaga, the big lake, which is often choppy and wind-blown, was smooth, reflecting the islands and mountains in its glassy surface. We paddled to the Canadian island across from American Point and camped for the night. The next day was cloudy, and we paddled through the southeast corner of Quetico Provincial Park in a cold rain. We made camp early that night and got the boys into their tents to warm up. A wolf howled off and on for several hours in the evening to entertain us.

The next day was cloudy and cold. No one wanted to paddle in cold rain again, so we declared it a rest day and spent the time reading, writing in journals, talking, and resting. I remembered earlier when the boys were discussing TV programs they missed, and I realized I hadn't seen a TV or read a newspaper all summer. I guess I didn't miss them. I noted in my journal, "I was thinking about TV and the effect it has upon so many Americans. TV gives people the feeling that they have experienced something, yet at the same time actually makes them lazier, so they experience less." We were certainly getting our share of experiences during this summer amid the northern lakes.

A day after I wrote this, the group was gathered around the campfire in the evening and got involved in a long discussion about literature. Since I was preparing for my first year of teaching high school English, I was eager to hear what both the counselors and campers thought. All the boys had stories and books they wanted to talk about, and that made me feel good. Their enthusiasm for the books was as high as the previous conversation we had about television.

The days of rain ended, and we left Elevation Lake in perfect paddling weather. Inspired by the warm sun, puffy white clouds, and the day of rest, we paddled all the way to Greenwood Lake and slept at the eastern end with our fire on a sand beach. Moose sign was abundant, as were the wild raspberries which topped our oatmeal in the morning.

We left Greenwood Lake and saved two portages by running short rivers, but paid for it on the next portage because a recent windstorm had blown down numerous trees. This area of Canada is not often traveled and is not part of a park, so maintenance is infrequent. We had to lift canoes and backpacks over downfallen logs, making it more work, but the boys saw it as a challenge and made a game out of it.

We paddled across Hew Lake and an unnamed lake beyond. There we found a narrow channel that let us glide through the swamps of water lilies and arrowroots. Prime moose country. Some time later, we got to run a series of small rapids in the canoes as we entered Trafalgar Bay.

At Northern Light Lake, we were casually paddling along, feeling good about making the loop up to Greenwood Lake. On a rocky point, we could see three men standing, watching us. They were the first people we had seen in five or six days, so we waved with a paddle, and they waved back. One man shouted, "Do you know what time it is?"

"No, I never carry a watch," I answered.

"We've been here for three days and haven't known the time."

"We've been here for two months and haven't known the time or the day of the week."

Chapter 7

The Marathon Feeling
August 5, 1993

Joe explained that it had been a cold, wet year in Bozeman with snow on the ground every month. We were seeing the effects of that wet year. The rain in the night. The heavy clouds on the snowy pass. The rushing streams. The muddy trails.

At one point, we saw a wooden sign that said 6.5 miles to the trailhead.

"We were so tired and exhausted that those six miles seemed like they took forever," Joe later said.

We had reached what I called the "marathon feeling." Everything was tired. The legs hurt, deeper than muscles, into the bones. Shivering in the rain with no sleep had left our minds aching deep inside as well.

When I lived in Jackson Hole, Joe had come to visit many times. On two of those occasions, we had entered a trail race called the Rendezvous Mountain Hillclimb. Rendezvous Mountain is the ski hill at Teton Village and the race, at that time, ran up the service road, gaining more than 4,000 feet to arrive at the aerial tram station. The trail is steep enough in some places that it is faster to walk than to run. The reward for running up was riding the tram down.

Those runs and our many hikes and climbs set us up to try a race called The Bridger Ridge Run, a course that follows the spine, from north to south, of the Bridger Mountains just north of Bozeman. In fact, it was this race that gave us the inspiration to try to complete our north-south traverse of the Crazy Mountains.

The Big Sky Wind Drinkers, the running club that sponsors the race, wrote on their web site, "The Bridger Ridge Run is one of the most technical trail runs in the United States. In 2012, *Runner's World* magazine named the Ridge Run one of its top thirty-one trail races in the country, giving it the title of 'Most Raw Exposure.' In 2013, Outside Online named the Ridge Run one of its Top 10 Bucket List trail runs in the WORLD. The Ridge Run is 19.65 miles of brutal climbing and descending, complete with unstable footing, unpredictable weather, and, of course, miles of exposure along the ridge line of the Bridger Mountain range."

With hype like that, the race today has become very popular and is restricted to 250 runners each year. When we ran it in 1990, we joined sixty other runners at the start line at Fairy Lake. After a very informal start, we set out and immediately climbed straight up Sacajawea Peak. The race course crosses other peaks including Saddle and Bridger, along with a series of lesser peaks as it sawtooths its way south to Baldy, home of the large white M on the hillside, honoring Montana State University.

Because the run is along the ridgetop, all water and food for the aid stations has to be carried in on horses or humans. It is a rugged experience, both for runners and volunteers.

Joe and I worked our way up and down peaks throughout the day. At last, we arrived at the M and made the steep descent into the parking lot below, finishing the Bridger Ridge Run in six hours and seventeen minutes.

Fortunately, Joe had a hot tub in his back yard in Bozeman.

By five p.m., the trail in the Crazy Mountains had become clear and the walking almost mindless. After three days above timberline, it was refreshing to be back in the trees. The meadows, with so much moisture, bloomed with alpine flowers. Bright green. Sharp colors. All wrapped in thick forest beneath granite peaks.

It was "a great splash of grandeur," as Steinbeck had said.

"I liked the whole concept of this trip," Joe recounted. "We intended to pack light and move fast. It was such a fun idea. No one had ever done this before, and I have never read about anyone doing anything even close to this in the Crazy Mountains. The goal of our trip was to traverse the entire length of the Crazy Mountain range from north to south by going over as many summits as possible."

That concept was gone.

Having abandoned our original plan (Could that decision have been made only twelve hours before?), we talked about that change. Yes, there was a hint of disappointment. We had talked about the trip for months. We had trained well and were in good shape. We had climbed for two days in near-perfect conditions. Then the rain. Then the wet ledges. Then the sleepless night.

Mountains can change plans so quickly, and months of preparation can be forgotten in a moment. That is part of the mountaineering game. It is the full package that makes the sport so intriguing. Climbers and hikers love to dream up new trips, then spend time researching and planning, gazing at maps and guidebooks. It also

The central peaks in the Crazy Mountains were far more challenging than expected. The rain and ice on these sharp peaks put an end to the plan of making a full traverse of the range. Photo by Steve Gardiner

means that climbers have to train diligently, both to be ready for a climb and ready for any problems that might arise. All that training takes place knowing that travel arrangements, weather conditions, team members health, and a host of other concerns could easily end a climbing trip. Climbers have to train, in case the chance is there. They have to show up and see what the mountain offers. It may be insight and joy, or it may be disappointment and misery. The unknown is the draw and solving the mystery the reward. The uncertainty creates the drama. As the trip approaches, the waiting becomes action. Planning becomes packing. Traveling becomes trekking.

Some trips go exactly as planned. Most trips require revisions. Adjustments are made and trips continue, sometimes, like ours, in a different, but still interesting, fashion.

As trips wind down, we have often found ourselves looking at horizons. What's next? Where should we go, and what should we do?

On our march out of the Crazy Mountains, we made no future plans.

In the early evening, we hiked for an hour in light rain and watched with some concern as the sky darkened. The urge to reach the car was strong at this point; however, the increasing rain forced us to duck under a stand of trees. Soon after, lightning followed.

Years earlier, Joe and I had paddled across Leigh Lake to climb Mount Moran in Grand Teton National Park. We found a good camping site at the base of the CMC route and settled in for the night. We left camp at six a.m., and reached the technical part of the climb at eight. The route climbs up a small summit called Drizzlepuss, then descends into the notch between Drizzlepuss and the East Face of Mount Moran. The route up the East Face is several pitches - rope lengths - of technical climbing. We took turns leading and moved quickly and easily up the sheer granite face. We arrived at the summit at ten a.m., much earlier than we expected.

We rappelled the main face, reclimbed Drizzlepuss, and climbed back down to camp. We didn't stay long because dark clouds were building and light rain was falling. We packed our equipment and walked down the lower gully, a steep and exhausting process, to reach the lakeshore and our canoe. Both of us had sore feet and toes by the bottom. We loaded the canoe and paddled onto the lake.

Soon after, the dark clouds descended and brought lightning. We did not like being in the middle of the lake in an aluminum canoe during a lightning storm, so we headed for shore. We were just entering the south arm of Leigh Lake, so we went to the western shore where a forested point juts into the lake. We landed, dragged the canoe up the shore, turned it over, and found a dry spot in the trees where we could wait out the lightning.

We sat in the trees at Leigh Lake for twenty minutes until the lightning stopped. Then, we pushed our canoe into the lake and paddled back on water as smooth as a glossy book cover. We had both climbed well that day, and we agreed that it was one of our best climbs together. It was very satisfying to see how quickly we had moved up the route, how efficiently we were able to climb and descend, how the climbing flowed like our free-fighting had during our Taekwondo training. That is the result of years of climbing together, knowing and trusting each other.

After the lightning ended in the Crazy Mountains, we resumed our hike to the car. By approaching our car from the north, we were seeing unfamiliar terrain, different from when we drove the car in to park it. We were unsure exactly how far to the car, but Joe kept us on track with a small-scale Forest Service map.

I did not know it at the time, but on August 13, 2011, some eighteen years later, I would return to the Crazy Mountains and complete a solo ascent of Crazy Peak, the highest summit in the Crazy Mountain range. It was a lengthy day involving a climb from Blue Lake, up through a band of very loose rock, ending with a climb through another deep notch like Joe and I had seen on the third day of our traverse of the range. Even though Joe had moved to the Tri-Cities in Washington, and could not go on the climb with me, standing on the summit of Crazy Peak made me feel like I had somehow finished the cycle.

Just before eight, nearly fourteen hours after we had left our ledges and more than thirty-six hours since we had last slept, we arrived at Joe's car. We changed into dry clothes, a luxury we had imagined all day, and drove to the north end of the range to retrieve my Jeep.

"When I remember this trip, I think it was a true test of endurance," Joe recalled. "We had to push for thirty-six hours with little food, no sleep, and the exhaustion that hypothermia creates. It was a major effort. How much can your body do when it needs to?"

We had hiked forty miles through glacial-carved mountains and most of that distance was off-trail while ascending and descending thirteen mountains. When we planned the trip, we had sought adventure, and we had certainly found it. In our modern world, where so little is left unknown, it was a treat to be walking where few, if any, people had before.

"When I got to my house in Bozeman, I kind of just rolled out of my car," Joe said. "That is the most exhausted I have ever been in my life."

A Moment of
Shock in Space

_____
_____

Chapter 8

Touching The Future
January 28, 1986

I woke up with a headache. I felt dizzy, and not long after standing up, I was in the bathroom vomiting. I was in my eighth year of teaching high school English and my first year at Jackson Hole High School in western Wyoming. There would be no teaching that day. I called the school, reported my illness, and outlined my lesson plans for the substitute.

Not long after, my wife Peggy left the house, taking our daughter Greta with her. With the house quiet, I fell onto the couch with a blanket. Whatever had attacked my head and stomach was going full force. I settled in for a long, uncomfortable day.

Somewhere in the haze of discomfort, I remembered that the Challenger Space Shuttle carrying Christa McAuliffe, the Teacher-in-Space, was scheduled to launch that morning. It had been delayed several times from earlier days as NASA made corrections and flight planners watched the unusually cool Florida weather. I turned on the TV and followed the coverage of the preparation. It was a welcome escape from my illness.

I joined millions of people from across the United States and around the world who watched that morning. We saw footage of Christa and the other crew members waving to the crowd as they arrived and prepared to board the Challenger. We saw views of the control room. We saw replays of the crawler transporting the shuttle to the launch pad. We watched clips about each of the crew members. We saw shots of the crowds who had gathered near the Kennedy Space Center to see the launch firsthand.

Christa, with her vibrant personality and her classic comment, "I touch the future. I teach," had captured the hearts of the public. Educators everywhere were proud of her and hoped her involvement in the space program would bring welcome attention to the teaching profession and the work being done in America's public schools. Thousands of TVs in classrooms everywhere were tuned in to witness the launch.

The countdown continued. After the previous delays, it was exciting to see the clock running. Then, at 11:38 a.m. Eastern Time (9:38 a.m. Mountain Time in Wyoming), the rockets fired and the Challenger lifted off.

The white smoke from the rockets shot like an arrow into the crystal blue sky. Then, suddenly, the line of smoke twisted, winding and splitting. The world held its breath and watched stunned. The Challenger had exploded.

The explosion, and events like the assassinations of JFK and MLK, the fall of the Berlin Wall, 9/11, and similar national and international moments give us markers in life, points of reference that we share with others. We often ask, "What were you doing when you heard Kennedy had been assassinated?" "Where were you when you first saw the images of the planes flying into the Twin Towers?"

We also do the same with personal events like births, deaths, and weddings. "That was before we had kids." "That happened after my father passed away."

Weather events serve a like purpose. "It was about the same time as Hurricane Katrina."

These are instants that lock themselves in our minds, that help us stake ourselves in history.

President Ronald Reagan announced the Teacher in Space Program on August 27, 1984. He wanted a program that was open to all teachers in the United States with the teacher that was selected to become the first private citizen to travel in space. The teacher would not be part of NASA's astronaut corps, but would be included on the shuttle as a payload specialist.

NASA mailed 40,000 application packets to interested teachers. Each packet required a teacher to provide background information as well as respond to a series of essay questions spanning nine single-spaced pages of writing. Applicants also needed to secure three letters of recommendation from a community member, a professional colleague, and a school administrator detailing their backgrounds and skills. NASA had accepted application packets between December 1, 1984, and February 1, 1985, and in the end, eleven thousand teachers took the time and energy to complete an application packet.

I was one of them.

Two teacher finalists would be selected from each state. Each state's Department of Education would set up a system to determine the two representatives. Wyoming had a committee at the State Department of Education that read all the applications and chose twenty semi-finalists.

On March 15, 1985, I received a letter from Lynn Simons, Superintendent of Public Instruction saying, "Congratulations! You have been selected as a semi-finalist in the Wyoming NASA/CCSSO Teacher in Space Program. You are one of twenty semi-finalists from a field of eighty-six applicants to be considered as Wyoming's representative in the national program."

Simons explained that my application would go on to a statewide screening committee which would determine the finalists who would go to Cheyenne for personal interviews. Those interviews were conducted the following week, and on March 26, 1985, I received a second letter from the State Department of Education stating, "The committee has completed its semi-finalist review and selected six finalists for personal interviews with the committee, as required by the project's guidelines. Unfortunately, your application was not selected by the committee for finalist status."

I had dreamed of being a Wyoming representative and attending the workshop at Johnson Space Center and meeting the other applicants going through the selection process. I knew being the Teacher in Space was a very long shot, but the workshop and meetings would have been a wonderful experience. My chance was over; however, the emotional expenditure I made to apply and anxiously await the results had invested me in the Teacher in Space Program. It made the impact of that explosion, which happened two thousand miles from my home, hit me hard. When I saw the twisting trails of smoke on the TV screen, I sat up on the couch. A fresh wave of nausea overcame me.

As soon as I heard about the Teacher in Space Program, I called for an application packet. When it arrived, I read through the criteria in detail. I met all the medical standards and physical requirements. I read about the essay questions. I had good ideas for every answer. I knew immediately that I was going to work hard on the answers and do my best on the application.

Those questions asked me to discuss my involvement in the community, my philosophy of teaching, and my communication skills. The main question asked me to describe what I would do for a Space Shuttle Special Project. By that time, I had been on a long list of adventure trips - rock climbing, mountain climbing, caving, snowshoeing, cross country skiing. Peggy and I had taught at the American School in Lima, Peru, for a year, and then we had traveled throughout South America and Europe. We had visited two dozen countries and found ourselves in some very difficult situations during those travels. I felt I had learned to adjust to challenges and unusual events.

During the adventure trips and my travels with Peggy, I also discovered how important keeping a good journal is. I had filled a stack of notebooks with the details of our travels. I wanted to record time, to place a value on how it was used, remember what had happened with it, and not just move through it.

Keeping those memories seemed important to me. Occasionally, I would dig out an old journal, one that was a year or two old and reread some passages. I found it interesting to compare what I recorded in the moment with what I pictured in my mind. Often, there were details that were altered by time, distorted in my mind until I corrected them with my own previous evidence.

I decided my Special Project would center on a journal that would portray the daily life aboard the Space Shuttle. Astronauts who returned from space were so deeply involved in the details of the mission that their reports were scientific treatises. I had never heard an astronaut really explain what it felt like to be in space, what the personal experiences meant.

With that in mind, I wrote, "The nature of a Space Shuttle mission is such that only a limited number of people can actually participate. Thus, it falls in line with other explorations which have a long tradition of journal keeping.

"Lewis and Clark could only take a select number of men on their journey across an uncharted America. Thor Heyerdahl, when he sailed across the ocean on his flimsy Kon-Tiki, had room for a handful of men. Sir Ernest Shackleton, in his attempt to reach the South Pole, had to choose thirty men from over five thousand applications. These and many other expeditions in history were limited to a few participants. Yet, because Lewis, Clark, Heyerdahl, Shackleton, and countless other explorers were avid journal writers, the experiences, emotions, and personalities of their historic journeys were not lost, but are alive for us and future generations to read, relive, and enjoy."

Not having been to space, I could only imagine what topics I would focus on for the journal. I made a list of ten to include in my application. They were

- The anticipation of space flight.
- The feelings on the launch pad.
- That first look at earth from space.
- The personalities of other crew members.
- Their reactions to their jobs, their motivations.
- Their comments on participating in historic events.
- Their emotions through the flight.
- The sky as a traditional philosophical stimulus.
- The feeling of being so far from home.
- The return to earth.

I felt that if I had access to the information about the daily lives of the Space Shuttle crew and experienced what the activities were, I could convey those details in a manner that would be readily accessible to large numbers of people. I explained that "overall public interest in space missions has declined in recent years, because the information has become more technical than personal. If the public knew the astronauts better as individuals, the interest in their activities would be high. It is like writing a good short story. The author must make the reader care about the main character, or that reader will not be interested in the action of the story."

I concluded by writing, "Rather than more scientific terminology, I think the public needs a concrete example in standard English of what constitutes the space experience. The results of one more science experiment will not affect the general public. But a well-written journal of the mission might. And helping the public to understand the space program seems to me to be the most important assignment for the Teacher in Space."

I submitted my application, knowing it would be one of thousands sent to NASA. Over the next three months, my papers moved through the Wyoming process and eventually stopped. I was fine with that. Writing the essays had been an interesting project. It had been fun to dream, to think about such an adventure. Then, on July 19, 1985, I received a letter from Terri B. Rosenblatt, Director of the NASA Teacher in Space Project, announcing that Christa McAuliffe from New Hampshire would fly on the space shuttle, and Barbara Morgan from Idaho would be the backup candidate.

Over the next six months, I read countless articles about Christa and Barbara, about the Space Shuttle program, and about NASA. The media was filled with coverage. Some accused Reagan of a political move. The teacher unions had backed Mondale in the election. Some felt the program was a public relations push for NASA. If so, it had worked, because national interest in Christa and the space program had soared. Anticipation grew as the date for the launch of flight 51-L drew near.

Sitting on my couch that morning watching the launch and eventual explosion of the Challenger Space Shuttle, I had no idea that twenty-three years later, Christa McAuliffe would again be a part of my life. In 1995, my family and I had moved from Jackson Hole to Billings, Montana.

I was teaching at Billings Senior High School and in 2008, I was named Montana Teacher of the Year. It was a huge honor and meant a year filled with events such as meeting President Bush in the White House and traveling to Dallas, Princeton, New York, Austin, and sharing these experiences with the teachers representing every other state, the District of Columbia, Guam, Marshall Islands, U.S. Virgin Islands, and the Department of Defense Schools. It had been a chance to get to meet some excellent teachers from across the country, get to know them, and share ideas with them. One of the highlights of the year was spending a week at Space Camp in Huntsville, Alabama.

During that week, we flew missions on shuttle simulators, listened to several speakers from NASA including astronauts, and learned more about the space program. One emotional highlight of the week was the chance to hear Grace George Corrigan speak. Grace is Christa McAuliffe's mother, and her presentation to a room filled with state teachers of the year was powerful. Grace told about Christa's childhood, teenage years, teaching career, and selection as the Teacher In Space.

Grace explained that Christa, when pregnant with her son Scott, had started a journal so he would know about his life. When Christa's life ended too soon, Grace did the same. She wrote a book called *A Journal for Christa: Christa McAuliffe, Teacher in Space*, and before she left her talk at Space Camp, she gave every teacher there a copy and personally signed each one.

In the book, Grace explained that many people had called Christa a hero. Grace agreed, but not because Christa had risked her life as the first private citizen in space, not because she had died in that effort, but because she had lived her life fully. Grace wrote, "Christa lived. She never sat back and just existed."

Grace noted that Christa was a normal person with all the fears, worries, and hesitations that implies. Grace was a proud mother, and rightfully so, and said Christa was really a hero because she "worked unceasingly, to become the best person she could be. She suppressed her fears and conquered life's challenges—the real, everyday challenges that we have all faced and that we will continue to face. She placed others before herself. She placed personal honor above personal gain."

Grace spoke to that room of teachers. There were tears and sadness. There were joy and laughter. There were awe and respect.

Some teachers, like me, remembered clearly the stories about Christa and that tragic day in January 1986. Other teachers were too young to remember, but were learning an important lesson about our country's history. Regardless of age, every teacher who listened to Grace Corrigan that day at Space Camp in Huntsville experienced an important moment in life.

Christa McAuliffe had been an ideal choice for the "teachernaut." She created more interest in education. She generated an excitement toward science and space. She fostered a feeling of goodwill about America.

After the explosion, the space program went into hibernation. Scientists had to analyze what happened. Dozens of reports were written about the fateful o-rings and the lack of an escape mechanism for the crew. Theories about the explosion sparked many debates.

The last moon landing had been in 1972. By the 1980s, the space program had become routine. Shuttle launches took place with little national fanfare. The Teacher in Space program was supposed to fire up the public about what the country was doing in space. It did. The nation fell in love with Christa.

The loss of the Challenger and its crew was devastating. The space program was put on hold and gradually resumed some activity, but nothing like before. In the days of John Glenn, many astronauts were household names. Now, three decades after the explosion, most Americans could not name one of the current astronauts. Few could name any of the present missions.

The image of the exploding Challenger is burned in my mind. It serves as a reminder of a personal dream, a reminder of a national dream, and a reminder of a day when I was too ill to teach allowed me to witness an event which left me sick in my soul.

A Moment of Heartbreak in Jackson Hole

_____
_____

Chapter 9

Those Missing 18 Minutes
March 2, 1994

Screams pierced the hallway. I rushed out of my classroom and heard a student yell, "Mr. Young is having a seizure."

Dave Young's room was just thirty feet down the hallway. He taught radio and TV classes, so his classroom had two editing rooms in the back. When I opened the door, Dave was on the floor inside one editing room.

A student, Craig Richison, was kneeling over Dave. Craig was talking to Dave, but there was no response. Craig said Dave had been sitting at the editing board, working on a video, when he put his head down on the table, then slid off his chair. Dave had fallen and landed with his back on the floor and the back of his head against the wall which forced his chin down onto his chest, making his breathing a sort of gasping, snorting struggle.

Dave's glasses were on the floor. I picked them up and put them on a desk. I told Craig we needed to move Dave, so he could straighten his neck. We lifted him forward into a sitting position, slid him sideways, and eased him back onto the floor so that his head and torso were out the door and his feet were under the editing board. His breathing seemed diminished, but he was no longer gasping.

Craig unbuttoned Dave's shirt while I moved over to check his left wrist for a pulse. Dave took a couple of short breaths, then stopped breathing. I felt his wrist. No pulse.

On my initial visit to interview for a teaching job at Jackson Hole High School, Dave Young was the first teacher I met. He taught broadcasting. I got the job and was assigned the yearbook and newspaper. As the journalism teachers, we would be working together to cover the school news. Our first conversation made it clear that we would have fun working together, sharing ideas about journalism and working with some of the same students. However, it wasn't just journalism that we had in common.

When Dave found out I was moving from Gillette, Wyoming, he wanted to know if I was familiar with Devils Tower. He said he had had a dream of climbing Devils Tower since he was sixteen years old. I told Dave about my climbs on the Tower, and before our first conversation was finished, we had agreed to find a time to climb Devils Tower together.

A new school. A new friend. A new climbing partner. I was off to a good start.

When Dave fell from his chair in the editing room, student Dustin Hollingsworth dashed from the room, screaming as he ran down the hallway to the main office. There he explained what happened, and Carolyn Swendsen, the secretary in the office, called 911. Seconds later, Kathy Kendrick, the school nurse, and Burr Storrs, the principal, arrived in Dave's classroom just as Craig and I lowered him out the editing room door.

Kathy immediately checked Dave's neck for a pulse. Nothing. She bent over Dave and began mouth-to-mouth breathing. She breathed a few times, then did chest compressions. I told her I could do the chest compressions, so we alternated with her doing the rescue breathing and me doing the chest compressions. She wanted to do one breath followed by five chest compressions. We settled into a rhythm and switched off smoothly. Twice I placed my hand on Dave's chest to see if it raised when Kathy did the breathing. It did.

Kathy stayed calm, professional. It set the tone for everyone else in the room. Although the situation was tense, no one panicked.

Jim Wilson, from the Wyoming Highway Patrol, came in the room and asked everyone to move back away from Dave. Unfortunately, there were still students in the room and outside the door, so teacher Peggy Gagnon took Dave's students to her classroom.

We kept the alternating rhythm going for three or four minutes. "The EMTs will want his shirt sleeve away from his arm in case they need an IV," Kathy said. Burr took a pair of scissors and cut the right sleeve off his shirt. From my angle at Dave's waist, I looked up at his face and neck. He seemed so purple.

By then, I had been teaching at Jackson Hole High School for nine years, interacting with Dave almost every day. He shared his classroom with Tom Ninnemann and the two of them were masters of puns. Laughter poured out of the TV and Radio room throughout the day. I was talking to Dave about his previous work for KSGT radio station, and asked him if he had ever worked for a TV station. "Yes," he said, "but I was born with a face made for radio."

It was no accident that Dave was teaching Radio and TV classes at Jackson Hole High School. His dad had worked in radio and Dave remembered "going to the station with him, sitting on his lap, cueing up records and getting commercial tapes lined up to play on the air. He let me push all the buttons. When I got older, he said I had the type of voice that would lend itself nicely to radio work. I had to get rid of my New Hampshire accent in order to speak on radio. My dad taught me to speak 'standard English language' in order to be successful in radio. I worked in every aspect of radio and television over the next couple of decades."

Dave earned a bachelor's degree and a master's degree from the University of New Hampshire in Durham and began his teaching career in Portsmouth, New Hampshire, in 1968. He taught band and choir there for six years before moving to Punta Gorda, Florida, where he taught for a year, before moving to Jackson Hole in 1975. He worked for radio and TV stations in Massachusetts, New Hampshire, New York, and Florida and was the news director for KSGT radio station in Jackson for five years. Broadcasting jobs had given Dave the opportunity to meet and interview President Johnson, Lady Bird Johnson, both Presidents Bush, President Ford, President Carter, and a host of other celebrities.

Working radio and TV also taught him some important life lessons. Once, Dave had been sent to interview a New Hampshire senator. Dave held to the back of the crowd of reporters. "I was too shy or scared or both to be assertive and push my way to the front to achieve the goal for which I was sent. When I returned to the station empty-handed, the director said, 'We don't pay you to be a coward. We pay you for results. Now go get the information I've requested or keep on driving home.' Wow! Right between the eyes."

Dave went back, and the meeting was still in progress. He pushed his way into the group and "got the questions answered on tape. I found out it was easier than I had expected. I let my imagined fears get in my way. It was one of the most important lessons I had learned for success, and I guess it was always in the back of my mind as a teaching tool as well. There were life lessons I felt obligated to impart to some students who were where I was once. This wasn't taught in Education 101 in college."

When Jackson Hole High School started the radio and TV program, the school superintendent recruited Dave to build the program. Dave's professional background in newscasting was a strong benefit for his students as they wrote and filmed a daily newscast for the school.

Dave's sense of humor, his smiling face, and his helpful nature were the things I knew best about him. Those traits made it harder for me to look at him, on the floor, unconscious.

When the EMTs arrived, I was relieved. They immediately hooked him to the heart monitor which registered nothing. The EMTs placed patches on Dave's chest and prepared the defibrillator. One EMT said, "Everybody move back."

They shocked Dave. He stiffened from head to toe. I was expecting more of a convulsion, but it was a single motion. We resumed CPR, but still got no response.

"We need to move him out of the doorway," the EMT said. "Let's get him into the middle of the classroom." I resumed chest compressions, and Kathy continued the breathing. At one point, Kathy saw movement on the heart monitor, but she soon realized it was the chest compressions that were registering.

The EMTs put Dave on an oxygen system. Kathy continued the breathing by squeezing on an Ambu bag which forced the oxygen into Dave's mouth. The EMTs wanted to do a second shock with the defibrillator. We all moved back, and they shocked him again.

At this point I remember Dave became very pale. No breathing and no pulse. The EMTs prepared to shock him again. "We are only allowed to give him three shocks," said the EMT. With the final shock, Dave vomited. Kathy turned his head, cleaned his mouth and throat, and resumed squeezing the oxygen bag. I bent over to continue the chest compressions, and I remember thinking, "My God, he's going to die right here in his classroom."

I had so much adrenaline pumping that I never once felt tired doing the compressions. I concentrated on pushing his chest and watching for signs of breathing. I was afraid of seeing him die, but did not feel uncomfortable or worried at this point. I knew we needed to keep going, so I focused on that. I felt fear, but I was determined to do whatever was needed to help the situation. I knew that when this moment with Dave was over, there would be heavy emotion, no matter what the result.

"Stop the chest compressions," Kathy said. "I think I hear something."

I paused. Dave coughed, then sucked in a deep breath of his own. He coughed a couple more times, and his chest heaved. That was what we had been hoping for. That was what we wanted so badly. I didn't feel like celebrating, because the situation was still too tense and unknown, but it was a sign of hope.

One EMT placed an IV in Dave's arm. Burr held the oxygen mask over Dave's face. We covered Dave with a blanket, slid him onto a backboard, then lifted him onto a gurney. He continued breathing on his own. We moved him out the door of his classroom, down the hall, and outside to the ambulance. We lifted him up, rolled him into the back of the ambulance, and shut the door.

I had remained calm and focused, but as soon as the doors of the ambulance slammed, I was pushed off duty. Reality crashed in. I turned away and walked down the sidewalk. I couldn't contain it anymore. I started crying. Hard. Dave, my colleague and friend, was hanging on the edge of death.

One thing I truly admired about Dave was his musical talent. He was the drummer in a band that played at the Stagecoach Bar in Wilson every Sunday night. He loved music. He loved to play. He loved to make people happy. As the drummer, he was the heartbeat for the band, the keeper of the rhythm, the monitor of time for the group. On this day, his rhythm had stopped. His time had appeared to run out. Then, against the odds, his heart was beating again. He would still keep time for the band.

I was standing alone at the end of the school parking lot when Officer John Daily pulled up in his police car. He got out and stood beside me. I told him briefly what had happened, and I remember saying, "It was so hard to watch that." We talked, then he gave me a business card and said to call him if I needed to talk more. He walked back to the building with me, and I went into Kathy's office. We were drained, exhausted.

Jim Wilson, the highway patrolman, stopped by and told us he thought we did an excellent job. That was nice to hear. He had been a big help by suggesting that we stop the bells and keep students in the classrooms. Because of that, we had no one in the hallway when we wheeled Dave out.

I had a lot of questions on my mind about what had happened, and Kathy was very helpful in explaining that Dave had not had a heart attack. He had had a cardiac arrest, a malfunction of the heart's electrical system sometimes called arrhythmia. A heart attack damages heart muscles. In a cardiac arrest, the heart just stops beating.

Kathy and I talked through the end of the class period. When it was time for third hour, I was walking to class with teachers Pam Tarantola and Linda Thorn. I was feeling so tense I wasn't sure I could teach. Linda offered to sit with my students, so I went back to the office and found Kathy. We walked to the library where school counselors Bill Keithler and Marcy Tepper were talking with a dozen students. There were three or four who were very upset. Kathy and I told them what we knew and what we had experienced. They asked some very tough and thoughtful questions, including one girl who asked, "If he lives, will he be the same?" That was the hardest one to answer. Of course no one could know the answer, and we didn't want to think about what the answer might be.

Just before Dave fell, his teaching partner, Tom Ninneman, had stepped out of the room and gone to the teachers' lounge to run photocopies. He had been in the lounge when Dave collapsed. When Tom heard what was going on, he ran back to the classroom. By then, the room was crowded with people helping, and someone asked Tom how to get ahold of Julie, Dave's wife. Tom went to the office and helped contact Julie, then realized that Julie might get to the hospital before the ambulance did. Tom ended up driving to the hospital and staying with Julie until they took her into the ICU to be with Dave. When the meeting in the library with the students ended, Bill came out to the cafeteria. I could not sit still. The events of the day were flashing through my mind. Bill suggested we go for a walk, so Kathy, Bill, and I, along with two of the students, went outside. We walked for several minutes. The sun was shining and warmed us. The March air was crisp and fresh. I now understood fully what it meant to breathe that air. It had a cleansing feel to it, exactly what we all needed at that moment. I could only hope that Dave had more time, that he would be around to experience more sunny days and fresh air.

We went back to school and had two more class periods to finish. I don't remember anything about those classes. I was worthless as a teacher. The only thing I do remember is that Burr got on the intercom and announced that he had received a call from the hospital and Dave was doing fine, and they were preparing him for air transport to Salt Lake City.

Chapter 10

Living and breathing
March 2, 1994

After school, I went straight home, changed my clothes, and set out for a six-mile run on the road through the National Elk Refuge. I still had so much adrenaline going that I was finished before I knew it.

When I got home, my wife Peggy, an elementary school teacher, and youngest daughter Denby were walking in the street. Denby ran up to me, and I held her tight. Peggy had heard rumors at school and her principal had taken her out of her room to tell her the story. I gave her my version. In the evening, I played with my daughters, but I could not get the images out of my head.

I went to bed, but could not sleep, so I got up to read. I was still so tense I couldn't relax. I was up until one thirty, even though Burr and Kathy had both called with news that Dave was doing well.

On Thursday, I was tired. The word from Salt Lake City was that Dave was on track for a recovery. I was still thinking about him continuously and reliving each minute of the event. I talked again with Kathy, and she explained more of the medical concerns. The day passed in a haze of unreality. I don't remember what happened on Friday.

Saturday morning I was working in the garage when Dave called from his hospital room. He sounded a little weak and congested, but otherwise fine. It was so good to hear his voice. It made me all the more excited to see him in person.

I couldn't help but review the events over the next days. I realized how tenuous our existence here is, and how quickly it can be gone. Dave came to work in the morning, and by second period, he was dead and revived. It is a thin line we tread. That made me look with different eyes at my wife and daughters. The time we have with our family and friends is so important.

While we were doing CPR, I was aware of the danger and very frightened that Dave might be beyond our help. However, I also knew we were doing the right things and kept optimistic about what might happen. Only later did I learn that the odds were stacked against us in such a situation. Kathy explained that Dave was her first CPR case who lived. After I heard that, I called my brother Keith who had been an EMT in a volunteer fire department for several years. I explained what had happened, and he said he had performed CPR five times, and it had never been successful. He also suggested that I should contact my CPR teacher to explain what happened. I did.

Just before Dave collapsed, Dustin Hollingsworth, the student who had run down the hallway shouting, had set up a video camera for an interview. He had just turned on the recorder when Dave fell inside the editing room and Craig yelled for help. No one thought about the recorder, but it ran for over an hour before Dustin returned and realized it had been on. He shut off the recorder, then gave the tape to Tom Ninneman for safekeeping. The video portion of the tape was insignificant because the camera had been aimed at the backdrop where the interview would have taken place. The audio portion of the tape captured much of what happened in the room that day. It became, in effect, an accidental journal, a timeline, of the event.

 In the days that followed, several adults from the school listened to the tape. As the school nurse, Kathy was interested in how we responded to the emergency. By using the tape, she discovered that we had CPR going on Dave in just under one minute after he collapsed. He had stopped breathing for five minutes, and the entire episode took about eighteen minutes to get him on his way to the hospital.

Eighteen minutes. So much emotion, so many thoughts, and so many decisions had been crammed into the time it takes to drink a cup of coffee.

It would take me two full weeks before I would have the courage to listen to the tape.

Dave was in the hospital in Salt Lake City for six days. We decided that Dave, as the TV teacher, would appreciate a video get well card from the high school. His students carried video cameras around the school, taping anyone who wanted to send Dave a message. There were heartfelt and sincere wishes for his recovery. There were jokes about past events. There were shared memories.

I went to the office to record a message. I didn't know what to say, but as I was walking, I reached in my wallet and pulled out my CPR class card. Then I knew what my message would be. When the student pointed the camera at me, I said, "Dave, I hate to tell you this, but I wasn't supposed to do what I did." I held up the CPR card. "This has expired."

When Dave returned to Jackson, Tom Ninnemann got the keys to Dave's Suburban which was still parked in the school parking lot. Tom drove his own car, and I drove Dave's. We parked in front of Dave's house. I was excited to see him.

We walked into his living room and hugged him. We talked for thirty minutes, and he wanted to show us his wounds. He opened his shirt, and I said, "I have seen that chest before." He laughed and showed us the scars from the "roto-rooter" as he called it. He also showed us his ribs. His chest was one black bruise. I remembered in CPR class they had said not to worry about hurting the person. "If you are performing CPR, the victim is, at that point, dead." I couldn't believe how happy I was to see Dave standing there, able to feel his sore ribs.

Three weeks after Dave's cardiac arrest, he came to school to attend a faculty meeting. There was so much happiness in the room. As part of the celebration, school secretary Robyn Jones had prepared two certificates that Burr presented at the meeting. He gave Kathy a certificate for the Hot Lips Houlihan Award. He gave me a three-foot-long CPR card with no expiration date. Dave's physician, Dr. Hayse, explained how rare it was for a person to recover as well as Dave had. We had seen something of a miracle.

Dave returned to Jackson Hole High School in the late spring and taught the final weeks of the school year. The next school year, two things happened that changed life for both Dave and me. First, my wife Peggy and I both got teaching jobs in Montana and moved our family to Billings, a seven-hour drive from Jackson Hole.

Second, Dave's father-in-law passed away, leaving Dave and Julie some property in downtown Jackson. The property needed remodeling, so Dave took a leave of absence from teaching to remodel the buildings. After one year, he had enough of the property rented that he could make a living from that. He decided not to return to teaching and spent another year finishing the remodeling work. By the time the work was done, he received an offer to buy the property, and he felt he could not turn it down. They sold and invested the money to provide income and fund their sons' college educations.

We still talked about climbing Devils Tower, but with the Tower an eight-hour drive from Jackson, Dave doing his remodeling work, and me starting a new life in Montana, it seemed to slide farther down our priority list.

On the day of his cardiac arrest, Dave was fifty-two. His sons were ten and eleven. I was thirty-nine and my daughters were four, eight, and ten. More than two decades have passed since that day, and we have stayed in touch by email, sending photos and stories of our lives and the developments taking place with our children.

"When I look back to see all that I would have missed, it is truly a miracle that everything was in place that day for me to be brought back," Dave said. "Otherwise, I would have been fifty-two forever. Some people may get all mental talking about an event like this happening to them, but I'm okay with it, because I'm glad to be alive to even discuss it. That's a good thing."

Dave told me he wanted to make the most of his second chance.

He said, "Every day I wake up in the morning, look around and say to myself, 'Wow! I made it through another night, and I have a chance to live another day. What good can I do today to help someone's life be a little better?' I will be the first to admit I don't always find ways to show it, but it is in my heart and mind constantly. Giving back to others is the only way that we can begin to repay the gift of life that we have been given."

He has made good use of his family time. I wrote to him once to explain a climbing trip I had been on in Greenland. He replied, "We too had a busy summer, and we also visited a foreign country... Boston." Dave was born and lived many years in New Hampshire, so the trip was a chance to visit his brother and family, as well as take his sons "to a Red Sox game at Fenway park, which my two boys dearly loved since I have brainwashed them into being Sox fans." They also traveled to Washington, D.C., and visited several Civil War battlefields, Monticello, Mount Vernon, and Atlanta. Over the years they have also traveled to China, Europe, Hawaii, Israel and Jordan.

Dave's son Michael loved Boy Scouts. "I went to the Philmont Boy Scout Camp in New Mexico with him once." Dave said. "We spent ten days in the wilderness, hiking nearly seventy miles during that time, camping, learning all aspects of survival in the outdoors that were taught by the leaders. It was a great learning experience for me, as well. Michael still recalls memories of that trip from time to time."

Dave had long had an interest in restoring old sports cars. He said, "I began buying them, tearing them to the ground, restoring them for driving and later selling them. I never made much of a profit, but it was the fun of creating something from scratch, driving it for a while, and putting them back on the road." Then, when his youngest son Jeffrey showed an interest in sports cars, the two of them restored a 1962 Austin Healey, and Jeffrey went on to a career in auto body work and restoration. Dave has restored two MGBs, a 1958 Chevrolet Impala, a 1959 MGA, a 1962 MGA and a 1957 MGA that he still drives around Jackson.

In 2003, Dave purchased a 1955 MGTF sports car on eBay from

a man in Miami. He wanted another car restoration project, so he and Julie decided to drive to Florida with a trailer and get the car. Jackson Hole winters can be rough, so they hoped to look around Florida as a possible retirement location. They drove to the Keys, but discovered it was not what they wanted. They headed back to Wyoming, driving along the Gulf Coast and through Texas and New Mexico before returning to Jackson Hole via Laramie where they got stranded in a blizzard. "That confirmed my pledge not to live in winter anymore," Dave said.

They liked New Mexico, so the next winter they drove back to New Mexico and headed west into Arizona where they stayed in an RV park in Tucson. They liked it. They drove their RV to Tucson for several years before buying a park model home where they spent four winters before selling it and buying a house. That turned out to be the retirement location they were looking for.

Music is often a form of time travel, a virtual time machine. We hear a few notes from a song and can relive moments from years, even decades before. We can picture where we were when we heard the song, who we were with. Those memories seem embedded in the song, even if the connection wasn't clear at the time the memory was formed.

Dave still plays his drums. In the summer, he plays with the Stagecoach Band in Jackson Hole. The band recently celebrated playing on 2,400 Sundays, and Dave had been part of that since 1986. In the winter, he is a percussionist with the Tucson Concert Band and with a small band from the RV park, and he sings in a barbershop group.

I once watched an elderly friend cross names off in his address book. He made a comment about it being difficult to keep living when so many friends had passed. Yet, we work hard at staying alive. We replace hips, knees, and heart valves, but our parts continually wear out. We keep ourselves breathing even though the extended time may mean facing the incapacitation of dementia or stroke. We battle with time, not so much that we want to live forever, but that we do

If things had worked out differently, "Look what I would have missed seeing for more than twenty years," Dave said. "We visited my son Michael in Longmont on the way (to Tucson). I would have missed having my adorable two-and-a-half year old blonde granddaughter run up to me, grabbing my hand and saying, 'Grandpa, come here. Come see this!' and seeing the look in her eyes while showing me her new doll. Priceless."

"I was always looking for adventures to make life interesting and fulfilling," Dave said. "Mountain climbing filled one of those niches along with playing music. I climbed Mount Washington in New Hampshire with my dad and oldest brother when I was twelve. Climbing up Tuckerman's Ravine was no small endeavor for a lad that young. I was also small for my age, but I was tough and wiry. I also had the determination to finish what I started. I have climbed extensively in the Tetons. I've done the Grand Teton twice, Mount Moran, and many routes on Mount St. John's. I never had the aspiration to climb Mount Everest, but I still loved climbing for fun."

When I first met Dave Young, we intended to climb Devils Tower together. It was our first connection. We talked about it. We wanted to do it. We talked about it some more. After I moved to Montana, we emailed about it. We never got it done. I would have loved climbing with Dave, but I am forever grateful he survived the events of March 2, 1994. He was the best climbing partner I never had.

A Moment of Childhood Play in Kansas

_____
_____

Chapter 11

A Game of 43-Man Squamish
Fall 1966

The ball was high in the air. As it fell, I realized that it was coming to me. I was excited. I set my feet solidly on the ground and bent both knees in a ready-position. I held my arms in front of me, palms up and elbows curved, forming a basket in front of my chest.

The ball fell into that basket, and I trapped it between my hands and chest. I quickly tucked the ball under my left elbow against my ribs and started running. Two opponents rushed towards me. The closest bent low, getting ready to make the tackle. I moved my head and shoulders to the right, then planted my right foot wide. That gave me leverage to spring left, like a bow drawn tight then released when shooting the arrow. I slipped sideways, and the tackler slid to the ground, his hand brushing against my right knee.

With my momentum heading left, I faced the second tackler. He had seen my movement to the right and wondered where I was going next. He hesitated just a fraction of a step, and with that hesitation, I used my own momentum to sprint around him, just along the edge of the sidewalk, and head down the grass toward the bushes by the driveway.

Making the catch and avoiding the first tackler had taken a short time, but it was enough to allow two others to cut across the yard and angle toward me as I ran parallel to the sidewalk. I knew I needed to get to the tree. I sprinted, hugging the ball close to let my arm move quickly through a short arc. Just as I reached the tree, I could hear the steps of two others closing from behind and to the right side. I reached out with my right hand, grabbed the tree trunk, and used it to spin. My speed whirled me around the tree trunk and sent me off directly toward the bushes. The two would-be tacklers, wide of the tree, were left gasping.

I slowed down, catching my breath and looking over the yard. Three others, who hadn't followed my line to the tree, were now approaching. They spread wide, forming a sort of barricade to stop my run. That left only the bushes, so I jumped over a low one, cut between two bushes, and hooked left. Four other bushes formed a line along the edge of the driveway. I used them in the same way a kickoff returner in a football game uses a wall of blockers. The three tacklers who formed the barricade were now blocked themselves. I ran around the bushes, and having reached the end of the yard, headed back, directly into the mob of tacklers in the middle of the yard.

There was no escaping this time. One wrapped both arms around my left leg. I pulled harder with my right leg, dragging him along the grass. Another tackler grabbed me around the waist just as a third pulled my right arm downward. We ended up in a pile of sweaty, laughing bodies.

We laughed a minute, caught our breath, and unraveled the pile. We stood up, and I took the ball, held it in both hands between my knees, and launched it skyward. It reached the apex, fell back to us, and landed in the arms of the next runner. I joined the pack in chase.

It was the purest form of sport. It was a game with no innings, rounds, periods, or quarters. There was no coin toss, no referees, no whistles, and no out-of-bounds.

In many sports, time is an essential element of the game. Players and fans can see the game clock running. They hope to speed it up or slow it down, depending on the score their favorite team has. Shot clocks or play clocks control smaller portions of play. During the game, coaches call timeouts. They pride themselves on clock management, especially in the late stages of an event. Eventually, time runs out, and the game is over.

When Intense Experience Shifts Time

In racing sports, time is everything. The fastest time determines the winner and individual places. Combined times or scores based on places identify the team champion.

These views of time are objective. We trust that the time of a game or race is accurate, often to tenths or hundredths of a second. We believe that records mean something, and that when a record is broken, the new time is definitely better than the old time.

Yet, we are also aware of a subjective time, a sense of time than can be altered by our perception of it. We even have common phrases such as, "Time flies when you are having fun," that reflect that subjective nature of time.

We seem to have an internal clock that goes beyond years and months, weeks and days, hours and minutes, and measures events in our lives based on our emotions, which can be affected if we are tired, cold, bored, frustrated, happy, or excited. Within the cycle of a game or race, the objective time, based on the ticking of a clock, is all important; however, in much of the rest of our lives, subjective time, our perception of the events we experience, is more important and leads us to understanding the events and our reactions to them.

A game was never scheduled. It just started at someone's suggestion, usually a few minutes after we all got home from school. The game required a ball--any kind--though a football seemed to be used most often, but a truly impromptu game could be played with a sweatshirt tied in a knot. After all, the ball was not functional, but symbolic. It identified the runner.

There was no face-off or jump ball. Someone, usually the owner of the ball, simply tossed it in the air, and the game was underway. When the ball came down, the person who caught it, or was standing nearest the spot where it came down, was the runner. He tried hard to catch the ball, because that gave him a head start. If he missed the ball, he would have to retrieve it, and that gave the rest of us a chance to catch up. Occasionally, a timid fellow would purposely miss the ball, trying to avoid being the runner. It didn't work. When the ball landed near him, he was the runner, ball or not. But those of us who loved the game, positioned ourselves, hoping the ball would come our way and give us a chance to be the runner.

When the runner had the ball, he would take off with the pack in pursuit. The runner could go anywhere he chose, and creativity could not only lengthen the time of being the runner, but could earn praise and respect from the rest of the crowd. Thus, it was fair game to use trees, wagons, bicycles, or cars as screens or blockers, and intimate knowledge of holes in fences or passages through thick bushes was a decided advantage.

Although deception was part of the game, nothing replaced a slippery sidestep or a diving tackle. This was a game, after all, of endless motion, of constantly flowing energy, and the object, though we likely couldn't have explained it at the time, was movement, the joy of play.

The runner kept the ball until he was tackled. Sometimes it was a matter of seconds, and other times, a particularly good run could last several minutes, but when the tackle was made, and the bodies unpiled, the runner would stand and toss the ball high in the air. With the briefest of breaks, the game resumed with a new runner and the ever-swarming pack.

Over time, the game went by several names like Tackle-The-Man-With-The-Ball, but one day, we saw a cartoon in Mad magazine depicting a game of mayhem called 43-Man Squamish, and that name stuck.

Time seemed much longer then. Of course, minutes, hours, days, and weeks are technically the same. They haven't changed, but internally, they are different. Many studies, based on the subjective reports of participants, have examined the idea that time moves faster as we age.

One theory for that is based on percentage. If you are ten years old, a year is ten percent of your life. If you are fifty years old, a year is two percent. That might account for some of our changing perception.

Another theory is that when we are young, we have more new experiences. There is more novelty, so we take in more information, and spend more time processing it. The memory created is richer and makes us feel like it filled more time.

As we age, more experiences are repetitive. We've been there before, so the routine makes it easier to process. With less things for us to focus on, our sense of time seems to slip by more quickly. That childhood summer, which seemed to crawl along, later takes to two feet and walks, then trots, and finally runs.

I have no idea how many times we played 43-Man Squamish. I don't remember if the games were just one summer or if they spanned two or three years. In my mind for half a century, it seems like we played a lot of times over an extended period, but we didn't keep any sort of records, so I will never know if my recollections are accurate. We didn't have calendars or schedules. We just wanted to play, to be involved. We wanted to be with friends and share a game where we were the ones in charge. We created the game. We developed the rules. We made choices when it seemed like a new rule should be added or what to do when a rule had been violated, although the way the game developed, it was somewhat hard to violate any rules. It was a sort of chaos, and we were in charge of it.

While I might not know how often we played or how long the game thrived in our neighborhood, I have strong memories of the feelings the game produced. We loved it. And we learned from it. We learned a lot about cooperation, and we learned a lot about physical motion.

Thinking back on those games, I realize that almost everyone involved went on to play junior high and high school football. We had inadvertently taught ourselves how to tackle and how to elude a tackler. We had designed a game that required a strong level of fitness, and we pushed each other to increase that fitness without ever setting that as a goal.

I played wide receiver and running back at two high schools. More than once, after making a reception or a run, I had memories of scenes from 43-Man Squamish. In college, I spent a semester at the University of London and joined the rugby team. With less experience than the English players, I was assigned to play winger, the person at the end of the line where I handled the ball less often, but got to make occasional long runs. In a game against the London School of Economics, I caught the ball, made a cut through some players, made a second cut through more, and scored a try. That run seemed to be a residual of the 43-Man Squamish games. Skills from our games of Squamish had crossed the Atlantic Ocean and had lasted many years after the small-town yards in Kansas had ceased to be our venues.

Although there were no teams, we needed each other to play the game. It was a contact sport with no pads or helmets, so we had to tackle and be tackled with a trust that we would take care of each other. We never tackled each other on a sidewalk or on a driveway or street. If the runner chose to head across the street, change the venue from Charlie's yard to Dirk's yard or Scott's yard, the pack simply followed, resuming the chasing and tackling when we were in the next yard.

We also helped each other corner the runner, cut off the distances, and warn of obstacles and screens. Even the runner needed the pack, because the pack presented the challenge and forced the runner to get better if he hoped to be the runner for long. Like many situations in life, the runner was against deep odds from all directions, and those odds frequently inspired brilliant performances.

There was no outside motivation for 43-Man Squamish. No one could win, and no one could lose. There was no way to score or be penalized. There were no rewards, except the fun of expending energy with friends, of laughing, of wrestling each other to the ground, of catching the ball and taking off ahead of the pack.

There were no buzzer-beaters, no two-minute drills, because time never ran out. Time didn't even exist when we played. After hours of grass-stained knees and bloody elbows, the game simply stopped. Perhaps someone's mother called from the front porch a few houses away, announcing dinner, her voice shattering the magic. Perhaps nature itself stopped us when it became too dark to tackle or catch the ball. Whatever the reason, the games ended with the same lack of fanfare and formality with which they began.

We walked home smiling and laughing. We were sweaty, thirsty, hungry, and tired but felt swept along in the flow of life. We would recall a particularly good run, relive a great tackle, and start thinking to ourselves about when we would play again. Sport couldn't offer more.

A Moment of Truth in the Andes

———————
———

Chapter 12

Climbing Nevado Pisco
July 19, 1982

I crept to the edge of the crevasse and looked down. It was a narrow crack, only three feet across at the top, so I could see down fifteen feet, then the curving sides created darkness and mystery below. I glanced at the snow on the opposite side. Since we were ascending, the other side was higher than where I stood. I would have to jump both out and up. It was not far, but a little awkward.

I took a few steps back, made sure there was some slack in the rope, took three quick steps, and leaped across the crevasse. I landed solidly on the crusted snow and moved on. Ten feet later, I faced another crevasse. The slope we were on was a jumble of ice blocks and crevasses, splitting the glacier in every direction. I jumped across that crevasse and landed on a flat, secure area. It was a good place to stop, set up a belay, and let Karl climb up to me.

"Karl, I'm safe on a good platform," I said. "Come on up. The belay's on."

"Climbing," Karl said.

I watched him wind his way up the slope, jumping over the same series of crevasses I had just jumped. He moved smoothly, efficiently. I had just met Karl two days before in the village of Huaraz in the Andes Mountains of Peru. We had agreed to climb Nevado Pisco together, but our planning did not include a route with this many crevasses. The conditions on the mountain were not normal, and we had both expressed concern about the broken nature of the glacier.

Karl climbed up to the flat area and stood beside me. He took a couple deep breaths. We were at just over 17,000 feet elevation, so the lack of oxygen was noticeable. After a brief pause, Karl continued upward, jumping over two more crevasses.

"The next crevasse is wider, but there is a snow bridge across it," Karl said. "It looks like I can walk across it."

Karl probed the bridge with his ice axe and moved slowly onto it. From my angle, it looked like the crevasse was six or seven feet wide. That meant he could probably see farther down inside the crack. While that doesn't necessarily make it more dangerous, it makes it appear more dangerous. He moved carefully, stepping gently onto the bridge. I let out just enough rope to allow him to move but tight enough to catch him quickly if the bridge collapsed. The bridge proved strong, and Karl walked across and continued winding his way through the crevasses. Some of the smaller ones he could walk around, others he jumped.

I had never been on a glacier fractured this badly. I had jumped crevasses and crossed snow bridges before, but never in such a concentrated mass. We encountered problems with each step. Every minute was filled with observations, discussions, and decisions.

I watched Karl climbing ahead. He was from southern Germany and had several years of climbing experience in the Alps of Switzerland, France, and Italy. He had told me stories about his climbs there, and as I watched him climb, he seemed confident. I felt reassured.

He reached another flat spot and set a belay anchor. When he was ready, I moved upward and continued the process of jumping over the gaps and walking on the snow bridges. I felt the gentle tug of the rope as Karl belayed it, giving me good protection on the precarious slope.

When I reached Karl, we looked at the glacier above. More fractures. More problems. We had been climbing for three hours, breathing the thin air, and needed a break before we tackled the chaos above. I looked at one crevasse about fifty feet above us. It appeared wider, darker than the others, and the upper edge was three or four feet higher than the lower edge. It was my turn to lead, and I needed a few minutes to think about that before I would have the

When Intense Experience Shifts Time 109

courage to attack that one.

My wife Peggy and I had arrived in Huaraz four days earlier. We had read about the village for months and had dreamed about traveling there. We wanted to visit the village and see the spectacular mountains of the Cordillera Blanca, the White Range, of the Andes Mountains that are just outside town.

We were working as teachers at Colegio Roosevelt, the American School in Lima. We had been living in Lima for four months, so we had grown accustomed to all the honking horns, screeching tires, and crowded streets and buses. In Huaraz, it was so quiet. That was what we noticed the most. We walked along the sidewalks, talked with the people, and enjoyed the bright sun. We knew the fog was heavy in Lima, but in Huaraz, Huascaran, the highest peak in Peru, dominated the skyline, completed the void in the end of the valley—the Callejon de Huaylas—and gave us a spectacular view of the Andes Mountains.

After two hours of walking through the streets and looking in the shops, Peggy and I stopped by the Hotel Barcelona, the center of activity for climbers coming into the Huaraz area. We planned to ask around for information about the routes, snow and rock conditions, and the possibility of finding other partners to join us on a climb. Huaraz, like much of Peru and South America was having a bad year for tourists, and consequently, we found no one at the Barcelona interested in climbing. We learned nothing about the routes or climbing conditions. We did find one note in Spanish and English posted by a climber who was looking for partners to accompany him on Nevado Pisco, a peak which has become popular because of its prime location between the mountains of Huandoy and Huascaran. I left a note in response.

That evening he came to the Hotel Andino where we were staying to meet us. He introduced himself as Karl Ritsert. He said he was eager to try a climb in the Cordillera Blanca. None of us had climbed in the area before, and as always, there is a concern about climbing in unfamiliar terrain.

Literature and history are filled with the stories of humans facing the unknown, and even in our modern times, the feeling is no different. That hesitation produces the anticipation, the adrenaline, that changes the act of climbing from one of pure physical work to an experience of life.

Unfamiliarity was furthered in this case by the fact that Peggy and I had not climbed with Karl before. I would have preferred a partner that I knew and had developed a trust-relationship with, but that situation was not available. New mountains. A new partner. If we wanted to climb, we would have to take what we had and go. What did the Andes have in store for us?

Peggy had had a head cold for the previous two days. In the afternoon she was feeling very ill. In the evening, she seemed better, and we thought she would be fit for the climb.

The packs were ready.

So were we.

In the morning, we met Karl, got a bus from Huaraz to Yungay, the tiny village nearest the park entrance. On the bus ride to Yungay, Karl, in his soft-spoken way, told us interesting stories of the two months he had just spent in Bolivia. We were lucky that his English was good, because our German was non-existent. His Spanish was also good. Intelligent and friendly, he was a special find for us in a foreign country. Isn't it interesting that we come from mountainous areas, and we met so far from our respective homes because of a shared interest, a mutual passion for the mountains?

The trailhead was at a series of lakes called Lagunas Llaganuco. To get there from Yungay, we would ride in the back of a truck. The driver told us he wanted to wait for enough people to fill the truck before he drove us to the lakes.

Being from the United States, Peggy and I were used to transportation that ran on a schedule. Karl, from Germany, grew up with transportation that moved with precision. We were patient with the truck driver, but finally asked when the truck might be leaving.

"*Cinco minutos,*" he replied. Five minutes.

OK. That's fine. We sat quietly and waited. Fifteen minutes. Thirty minutes. An hour. We asked again when the truck would leave.

"*Cinco minutos.*"

There are cultural differences in time, and we were seeing one in action. Our concern was moving toward the mountains, the sooner the better. His concern was filling his truck. His answer to our query was one he had learned would keep Americans and Europeans hanging around, hoping it might be true, yet give him the chance to add more paying customers to his truck.

When the driver had enough passengers in his truck, he started the engine and steered it toward the lakes. In the back of the truck, we had a great view of the peaks of the Cordillera Blanca. We drove up the valley just to the left of Huascaran. Climbers are always dreamers, and we gazed at the magnificent peak. We imagined its ridges and couloirs. We envisioned the summit and its view. Maybe someday we would return to give that one a try.

The first half of the trip was all Huascaran, but after the park entrance, other snowy giants took their turn on stage, and we felt like small specks in an other-worldly environment. Green lakes. Vast meadows. Vertical rock. Jagged ice. Land of awe.

Everyone in the truck was silent, as if we were all being absorbed into the expansive beauty surrounding us. The truck crawled along, but we didn't mind. We were in no more hurry than the mountains and rivers, than the sky and clouds. We were keeping time with the universe.

The driver took us directly to the trailhead. We unloaded our packs, ate a quick snack, and set out on a well-defined trail. At the end of the box canyon, the trail switchbacked up and exited to the left over a pass. Through there, we found a *pampa*, a high altitude meadow, with a house and a herd of cattle. These people were living at nearly 15,000 feet. That is higher than the tallest summit in the continental United States.

Another five hundred feet of climbing brought us to the lake at the base of Pisco. All around the lake are the rocky deposits of ice-age glaciers. In the midst of these moraines, previous climbers had scooped out level tent sites. We took advantage of one of them.

Karl had no tent, but used a bivouac bag just outside of our North Face dome tent. It had taken us four hours to hike to base camp. We arrived at six p.m., set up camp, and cooked in the dark.

On the hike in, Peggy had to drop back. She wasn't feeling well at all, so I walked with her. Her cold persisted and had weakened her. We doubted if her cold would improve at 15,800 feet, so we discussed alternatives for approaching the climb. We decided to climb higher, set up the tent, and leave the gear with her there. Then Karl and I would try the glacier. Karl had walked fast on the trail to the lake. I wondered if I would be able to stay with him on the climb.

Climbing is often a big puzzle. It all makes sense when the pieces go together, but getting them in place is often extremely difficult.

We rose before sunrise, ate, and scrambled up a large boulder field to a massive bench, then up a river gully to a flat ledge just below the glacier at 16,500 feet elevation. That was a good place to pitch the tent. We made sure Peggy was comfortable and left her there with our extra gear. Karl and I headed for the summit.

We followed the top of a morainal ridge toward the glacier, hoping it would connect. It didn't. We had to drop and reclimb three hundred feet and then climb two hundred feet more to reach the glacier.

Karl led an incredible ice escarpment thirty-five feet high just to get onto the glacier. Twice his crampons lost purchase and grated against the rough ice. At last, from behind an ice wall, he belayed me securely, and I struggled up.

As I climbed, I saw patches of blood on the ice, and when I crested the ice ridge where Karl sat, I saw his hand. Ice as sharp as a knife had sliced the knuckles on all four fingers of his left hand. Blood was dripping into the snow at his feet. He bandaged the cuts. I gave him my extra pair of wool mittens, and we continued our climb.

Ahead of us was an astounding maze of broken glacial blocks, seracs, crevasses, and steep snow. We would climb a rope length, stop and discuss how to pass a crevasse or how to climb over or around a frozen obstacle. Ice falls cascaded down the mountain on both sides of us. Jagged chunks of ice, icicles, spires, and gaping crevasses were everywhere.

We jumped over the black holes, slowly crossed the snow bridges, waded through thigh-deep snow, and balanced on steep icy slopes. Many times we overcame one obstacle only to find another just behind it or around it. We climbed and turned and jumped and dropped and climbed some more. Every step brought new angles of beauty–new perspectives of the alien world we were discovering.

If the glacier wasn't pretty enough, all we had to do was look in any direction. Below us were the glacier, the curved spine of the moraine, the yellow tent where Peggy waited, and the crystal blue lake in the valley, curving to the right and west toward Yungay. Straight ahead was the summit of Pisco. To the left were the four summits of the Huandoy massif. To the right was the impossibly severe Chacraraju. Behind us were the double summits of Huascaran and the symmetrical wonder of Chopicalqui. Any one of those peaks alone was beauty defined in concrete form. Together they were overwhelming.

We found it harder to breathe. I had only been at this altitude once before, and for Karl this was his highest. After half a day of climbing, we were no longer fresh. Even though this was exactly what we wanted, why we had come here, rest stops became more frequent.

At 18,000 feet, we paused, and I thought about the bigger crevasse above, wondering if I would be able to find a way over or around it. By then, our water supply was low, so Karl readied his stove to melt snow. He filled the pot, and we ate while the snow sizzled.

After ten minutes, the pot was filled with water. We decided to give it another couple of minutes to get hotter. The stove tipped. Water splattered on the food sack and instantly disappeared into the snow. We looked at each other, knowing that precious water had been lost and treasured time wasted.

Karl tried to re-light the stove. It wouldn't. He opened the fuel cap. No gasoline. The extra bottle was in his pack in the tent with

Peggy. No water. Not enough time. A biting cold wind reminded us too vividly of the hot water we almost had. No choice. We had to retreat.

I looked up at the black crevasse above. I would never know if I could lead it or not. We took as many pictures of the ice, the rock, and the panorama as our fingers could stand, quickly repacked our gear, and plunge-stepped down the tracks we had made on the ascent.

Backing off a climb is not easy. Time, energy, and emotion are invested in an attempt to combine a good experience with the chance

Karl Ritsert pauses at 18,000 feet on Nevado Pisco to heat water with Chacraraju in the background. It had taken so much time and energy to climb through the jumble of crevasses that we decided to turn back at this point. Photo by Steve Gardiner

to stand on a summit. We did not reach the top that day, but we had both received an introduction to the Andes and had a memorable experience. It would be impossible to feel regret about a peak which had given us so much.

Our descent was a happy one, though not carefree. We belayed the snowbridges and crevasse-jumpings as we had done going up. Many climbing accidents happen on the downclimb when a party has relaxed assuming the climb is over. We would not, and did not, make that mistake.

On the steep descent off the foot of the glacier, Karl thought enough to leave one of his axes placed with a carabiner attached to provide one point of protection for me. A kind and intelligent gesture.

We followed the moraine back to where Peggy sat in the sun reading a book and waiting for us. We packed the tent and gear, and hiked down to the base camp lake. We rejoined the nicely-constructed trail, walked down to the large *pampa* which proved too wet for camping, and finally pitched the tent next to a stream at the base of the switchbacks in the box canyon. From the three sides of this box, five separate multi-level waterfalls tumbled into the valley. Their roar and the increased density of oxygen provided our little-needed sleeping tablets for the night.

In the morning, we reached the lakes in an hour where we received terrible news. We talked with a French party that spent the night in the stone shelters at the lakes. One of their members, a woman, died of heart trouble during the night, and her body was inside the shelter. They had contacted the authorities at the park entrance station and were waiting for someone to investigate before they could remove the body. They would have to wait, maybe for hours, for the authorities to arrive. I shuddered to think of all the difficulties they would have, the language barrier, the paperwork, the transportation problems, all stacked on top of the emotional burden of losing a friend. They had come to the lakes for the natural beauty, enjoyment, and confrontation of the unknown—just as we had—and they had paid a tremendous price for it.

Two of them entered the shelter and returned, tears in their eyes. I couldn't look at them. Our experience had been good and contrasted so dramatically with theirs. Another chapter in our introduction to the Andes.

In camp the night before, Karl, Peggy, and I had talked about climbing in the Alps and about climbing in the States and how different it is from the Cordillera Blanca. The dimensions in the Andes are beyond any imaginings we had in our home climbing grounds, and with that increase in dimensions comes an increase in challenge, an increase in meeting that challenge, and a disproportionate increase in the dangers involved in the sport. The Andes appear as a world set apart, a world of their own, with a different set of rules and codes. They are immense, powerful, beautiful, and dangerous.

My curiosity about the peaks of the Cordillera Blanca had been justified. They are worth every bit of consideration a climber can give them. Our first Andean climb had been all we wanted. It provided us with a varied experience, a new friend, and a close look at a different place and lifestyle.

Waiting for the truck back to Yungay, we talked about the glacier on Nevado Pisco. Crossing the snow bridges and jumping the crevasses had pushed me into a new realm, and the images in my mind were powerful.

"I just want to thank you," I said to Karl. "When we were up there in the middle of that jumbled ice, I was pretty nervous. I had never seen anything like that. Knowing about your experience in the Alps and watching you climb made me feel confident that we were OK."

Karl turned to look at me. "Really? That's not right. I have never climbed in conditions that difficult. I knew you had climbed in the Tetons and on Mt. Rainier and that made me believe you were comfortable with what we were doing. That's why I stayed with the climb as long as I did. It seems we created a sense of security for each other."

A Moment of Tumbling on Molt Hill

———————
————

Chapter 13

A Dozen Seconds To Live
June 10, 1996

Second 1

I had turned my bicycle around at the seven-mile marker on the Molt Road west of Billings, Montana. The first six miles were flat or gently uphill, but the final mile was a steep climb. My quads had burned up that section, but they had recovered quickly. The weight lifting, running, cycling, and walking had paid off. The foundation was solid, ready for action. I had a series of mountain climbing trips planned for the summer. This level of training would make those climbs safer, more enjoyable, more likely for success. It was a good feeling, a sense of accomplishment and a stronger sense of anticipation. At age forty-two, I was completely ready for the challenges. I had nineteen years of climbing experience in North America, South America, Europe, and Asia. I had experience in rock climbing, ice climbing, and mountaineering, and my summer plans would likely call on all that background training. It felt good to be on the edge of adventure. I took a deep breath and stopped pedaling.

Second 2

I was at the crest of Molt Hill. It had been a good workout riding up, but now, poised at the top of the hill, I was ready to coast back down. It would be good payback for the work of getting up the hill. I would let myself coast to the curve near the bottom of the hill, give the legs a chance to rest and recover, then pedal hard to my home.

Earlier in the day, I had gone to the gym for an hour of swimming and half an hour of weight lifting. The fourteen-mile roundtrip on the bike would have me on the road for a bit less than an hour. It would round out a good day of training. I planned to spend some of the evening sorting climbing equipment for the next expedition. I leaned forward, dropping my hands to the lower level on the handlebars. Less wind resistance. More streamlined. A little fun and excitement to balance the strenuous workouts.

Second 3

Speed came quickly. The bike tires hummed on the highway. Although the day was calm and still, my downhill motion created a wind in my face. It whistled around the edges of my helmet, sending cooling relief into the ventilation holes along the top. It vibrated the excess end of my chin strap. It blew around the frame of my sunglasses and caused a tear in each eye. I blinked and the tears squeezed out the corner of my eyes. Because I was leaning forward on the handlebars, my face was parallel with the road, so the wind forced the tears down the sides of my cheeks and into my beard. My shoulders flexed to support the weight of my torso and head. My legs relaxed, feeling light on the pedals. The metal poles with reflectors marking the edge of the highway flashed past me. The asphalt churned into a blur as I hugged the white line.

Second 4

I would guess I was going twenty-five miles per hour. I was focused on the road immediately in front of me, but tilted my head higher to look farther down the road. A silver sedan was driving in the other lane about halfway up the hill. There was seldom much traffic on the Molt Road, making it a good place to ride a bike. I usually saw only a handful of cars in an hour's ride. Just as I glanced up, a second car, a Jeep CJ, pulled out from behind the first car to pass. That put the Jeep in my lane going uphill. Even though I was far right against the white line, the road was narrow. With the sedan in the right lane, the

Jeep had limited room in the left lane. With me going downhill at twenty-five miles per hour, and the Jeep going uphill at forty-five miles per hour, we approached each other in an instant. The gap closed so quickly that I had no time to think. I felt my entire body tighten. A jolt of adrenaline shot through me. One thought flickered through my mind, "I could die right here."

Second 5

A body in motion tends to stay in motion, the physicists tell us, until that motion is met with some other force or opposing motion. With gravity fostering my downhill motion, the laws of physics gave the mechanics of my bicycle little or no chance of stopping me safely in that instant left in front of me. A thoughtful response to my situation would be to grip the right brake which stops the rear tire. Holding tight to that and then eventually angling into the ditch, if necessary, would have been a good choice. However, with me coasting downhill and the Jeep accelerating to pass going uphill, there was no thoughtful response. There was no thoughtful anything. There was only adrenaline. Reaction. Fear. Deep panic. I crushed the brake levers with both hands.

Second 6

Squeezing the left brake lever had applied pressure to the front tire. Being left-handed, I may have even grabbed it tighter than the right one. The combined weight of my body and the bike flying downhill rolled over the front tire. I was like a pilot ejected from a fighter plane. I shot up and forward, airborne, and launched over the handlebars. The physics of slowing down my bicycle tires did nothing to slow me down. I flipped. The rear tire followed me over the front tire. For a nanosecond, it must have balanced with me and the rear tire fully above the front tire, before bike and body were rocketed skyward. I lost all sense of direction. I had no idea where the two cars were. Now gravity would shift its focus. Instead of rolling me smoothly down the hill, it was going to drive me into the pavement. It is amazing how a tenth of a second can explode.

Second 7

A friend of mine who races bicycles told me he had been knocked off his bike twice in accidents. Both times, the first thing that hit the ground was his head. That convinced me to wear a helmet every time I got on my bike. Now, suspended in midair, I did not think about having a helmet on, but with my feet inside the toe clips on the pedals, I traced an arc over the front tire and headed down. Indeed, my head hit the highway first. The crash of my helmet on the pavement was deafening. The impact cracked the top of the helmet in three places. Gashes in the top of the helmet suggest I skidded on my head. My neck must have compressed under that force, but it seems to have stayed straight. I don't know if my inverted body actually bounced on my head or merely somersaulted, but forward progress continued.

Second 8

I rotated off my head and landed on my back, grinding into the pavement. With only a sweaty t-shirt between me and the asphalt, I quickly collected what cyclists refer to as road rash. The area from just behind my shoulders to the middle of my back was filled with gashes and scratches. By initially landing on my head, my helmet had taken the hardest blow. By the time I turned onto my back, I was moving along the surface of the highway, rather than down into it. The sliding nature of that part of the fall kept the cuts superficial. It looked like someone had made several passes with a wood rasp up and down my back, especially around the shoulder blades. The contact between the flat of my back and the road created enough friction that momentum sent my head and shoulders forward, full circle from seated on the bike to now seated and sliding on the highway.

Second 9

The skidding tore my shorts and peeled skin off my butt before I stopped. The back side of my body, top to bottom, was burning from the scrapes. Somewhere in the violent tumble, my shoes had come out of the toe-clips, releasing me from my bike and it from me. I expect that, as I landed on my head and rotated forward, the bike went sailing on its own. It hit the road upside down, the saddle striking first. With little give, the seat ripped to shreds, sending the bike bouncing down the highway. It ended up lying on the shoulder of the road about fifteen feet farther than me. The handlebars were scratched, the brake levers roughed up, and the paint in several places chipped. No serious damage. With a new seat, the bike would heal much faster than I would.

Second 10

Somewhere inside the forward flip I had just taken, I heard the distinct sounds, the Doppler Effect, of the Jeep engine quickly approaching, zooming past, and racing into the distance uphill. The engine, paired with the clattering sounds of the knobby tires, emphasized how close the Jeep had been to my tumbling body and bike as it roared past. I will never know (and probably don't really want to know) how close the Jeep was to me at that split-second. Somehow, the driver had managed to slip between me and the silver sedan. Then I was lying on the road on my back. No more bouncing. No more engine noise. No more skidding and scraping. No more motion. Just silence. Quiet. Pain.

Second 11

My body was burning. The road rash was extensive, but the residual adrenaline tempered the pain. I sat up again and felt a stinging in my right hand. Somewhere in the cartwheel, my right hand had hit something, probably the road. The ring finger and pinky were cut, deeper than the road rash, and blood was dripping onto my leg and the highway. I wondered what else was damaged and began a quick checklist of pain and parts. I stood up. Nothing was out of place and every joint was able to function. Yes, there was pain. The road rash felt like fire, but nothing more serious had occurred.

Second 12

In a normal day, seconds are ignored. They seem unimportant, but on this day, when I assumed I was one second from death or tragic injury, each second was a gift. I thought I had one second to live. Then suddenly, I had thousands, millions of seconds. Having tread so close to death, I was overcome by the colors and smells of Molt Hill. Every sense was alive and vibrant. Even the blood and pain were welcome reminders of living and understanding that I was going to continue living, at least for that day. I was miles from home, but knew that when I returned, my wife and daughters would be there. We would have the opportunity to pursue our plans and dreams.

A Moment of Altitude in Argentina

———————

———

Chapter 14

Top of South America
January 29, 2005

Sometimes an adventure begins before the adventure begins. Such was the case for the 2005 Top of South America Expedition.

We had put together a team who had shared many trips before. There is a comfort in seeing familiar faces when we head off to remote regions of the world, so the list of names was reassuring. However, in the final weeks of preparation, Joe Sears and Terri Baker were forced out of the trip for medical reasons. With Terri out of the trip, her husband John Jancik decided to stay with her. David Baker took a new job, and Jim Schaefer was in the final stages of building a home, so they chose to stay behind. Of our group of returning climbers, only Vernan Tejas, who had been on the 2001 Top of the World Expedition to Greenland, and I were left on the roster. We were joined by Jen Pauley, Marshall Kettner, Jacob Artz, Paul Konicek, Hal Harper, and Pete Shelley.

I had worked one summer at an outdoor shop in Billings with Pete, and we had talked a lot about climbing, but had only spent one day outdoors together, climbing a frozen waterfall above Red Lodge, Montana, in the Beartooth Mountains. We would be tentmates on the Top of South America Expedition, and I looked forward to getting to know him better.

While I was excited to be climbing with Pete and making other new friends, it was unsettling to think about going on a major expedition without Joe and John. We had been on so many significant trips together that it did not seem right to pack my bags and head out without them. Sometimes life interrupts our plans.

The pre-climb troubles did not end with roster replacements. Because we were headed to the southern hemisphere, we would be climbing in late January and February. We arrived at the airport on January 29, only to learn that hundreds of flights across the nation had been cancelled because of a massive ice storm in Atlanta. That whole region was shut down, but we were able to reroute our flights through Los Angeles. We flew from L.A. eight hours to Lima, Peru, sat on the runway for over an hour, then flew on to Santiago, Chile, a total of fifteen hours in the same airplane. From Santiago, it was a short flight to Mendoza, Argentina, where we would set out to climb Aconcagua, at 22,841 feet, the highest peak not only in South America, but in both the Southern and Western Hemispheres.

We hiked two days up the dry and dusty Pampa de Las Leñas valley. We carried day packs with water and other essentials, but our heavier bags of clothing and climbing gear were hauled on mules. The trail to Aconcagua is paved in sharp stones, too sharp for horses' hooves, but the mules handle it well. The mule drivers, called *arrieros*, have learned to handle the stubborn pack animals. Each morning, they bring the mules into the middle of camp and place a blanket over their faces. When the mules can't see, they become rigid, like a statue, and the *arrieros* tie on loads of one hundred twenty pounds each. Once the loads are tied on, the mules seem fine and walk calmly up the trail.

After two days in the Pampa de Las Leñas Valley, we turned left into the Relinchas Valley where we found waterfalls and gorgeous views of Aconcagua dominating the upper end of the valley. Vernon looked up at the mountain and pointed to a vast snow ledge called The Edge of the World. "We'll be standing on that ledge and looking down in a week," he said. "Then you will know why it is called The Edge of the World."

I stood there, looking up at the The Edge of the World. Here I was in one moment, yet projecting myself ahead a week, imagining the view from that snowy ledge, and at the same time, wondering how

When Intense Experience Shifts Time

On the second day of the approach, we got this view of Aconcagua looking up the Relinchas Valley on February 4, 2005. Photo by Steve Gardiner

a ledge I could see ahead of me could possibly take a week for us to reach. Perhaps that is one thing climbers enjoy is planning for the future, taking a sense of control of time by preparing for it.

The psychologist William James said, "We are constantly aware of a certain duration – the specious present – varying from a few seconds to probably not more than a minute, and this duration (with its content perceived as having one part earlier and another part later) is the original intuition of time."

That we can perceive a present moment that is constantly changing, and at the same time remember past events and project ideas and plans into the future, is a sort of time travel in the mind, a gift that is uniquely human.

Since we arrived in Mendoza, we had heard stories of bad weather and storms pounding the climbers already on Aconcagua. I was concerned. Then, as we walked up the Relinchas Valley, we saw the results of those storms. We passed several groups who had been beaten back. They looked tired, disappointed. One man walked by, carefully cradling his hand, the frost-bitten fingers wrapped in white gauze. This was not the welcome we had hoped for on the mountain whose name means "The Stone Sentinel."

We arrived at Base Camp and spent an extra day resting from the thirty-mile hike in and sorting our equipment to begin our push up the mountain. The weather seemed better, and we could only hope that we would not face the nasty storms the previous groups had seen. We loaded our packs, and on February 6, we carried our first loads up to Camp I at 15,400 feet. When we arrived, we sat down on some flat rocks to eat lunch. The sun was behind Aconcagua, and we could see the shadow of the peak stretching out for miles on the landscape below us.

Two other groups had arrived ahead of us, so we set our camp a bit lower in a rocky bowl that would give us some protection if we did have wind. It would let us camp by ourselves and not be distracted by the other groups. It had the added benefit of being near a series of sharp rock and ice spires called *penitentes*. They formed a beautiful backdrop for our temporary community, and they prompted thoughts of geological time.

Aconcagua formed as a volcano, extinct now for more than nine million years. Comprehending the vastness of time required to form a mountain as massive as Aconcagua strains the fibers of any human mind.

We built a rock wall to house our kitchen and stored the food and equipment inside. We would go back to Base Camp for a good night's sleep, then carry another load of equipment and our tents up the next day. As we were setting up camp, a group passed us going down. They had had to spend three days stormbound at Camp III at 19,200 feet. Their faces were haggard, their voices weary. We were working under a sunny sky, so I felt confident that we would be fine, but an expedition to a mountain as big as Aconcagua will always create questions, make us think about our motivations and goals.

I had decided to make myself drink four liters of water each day. That is not an easy task, but dehydration on a big mountain can cause many problems. So far, I had been able to keep up that pace, and I was feeling strong and healthy. Eat well. Drink well. Sleep well. That was my plan.

Also, our plan to carry equipment to Camp I, then sleep at base camp was part of our acclimatization process. Each day we spent at the higher elevations on the mountain, our bodies were changing, producing more red blood cells and making other internal adjustments that would allow us to live and work at those elevations. While our spirits wanted to race up the mountain, we knew we needed more time to adjust. The double-carry system we would use, in addition to allowing us to carry reasonable loads, helped us make those important changes.

After we arranged our equipment at Camp I, we returned to Base Camp.It had taken six hours to do the hike up and down. We were all moving well, and everyone seemed in good spirits. We still had a lot of mountain above us, however.

There are library shelves filled with books about expeditions. The history of mountaineering, polar exploration, and other adventures is rich with stories of humans willing to take on difficult tasks, to push into the unknown to satisfy a curiosity, an urge to explore. We were no different. We wanted to know what it was like to climb high on a major mountain. We wanted to know what it was like to step out of normal life and live as those early explorers had done.

The accounts of reaching the North Pole, the South Pole, the summit of Mt. Everest have held readers spellbound. Those of us who have read those books learned about their determination, their ability to dream big and live those dreams. We watched them set a goal and stick with it through the long, difficult efforts that made marks on history. By sharing a connection with those expeditions, we become a part of the history of adventure, and we mark points in our own lives by giving our time and energy to projects that expand our lives and tie us to history.

We repeated the two-day process of moving food and equipment to Camp II at 17,800 feet, and then another two-day process to get everything we needed to Camp III at 19,200 feet. When we reached Camp III, we voted for a rest day. We had been double-carrying loads for six days and needed a break if we were going to continue strong to the summit. We slept in, ate a late breakfast, then took a short walk over to the broad ledge called The Edge of the World which Vernon had pointed out to us from the trail in the Relinchas Valley. We cautiously approached the edge and looked over. It was a straight drop of over 5,000 feet, a vertical mile to the valley floor. Small knots formed in my stomach, and a tingle surged up the back of my neck.

These days of carrying loads and setting up camps were also good for team building. During the hours of climbing and establishing camps, we had plenty of chances to talk, to get to know each other. Each night in our tent, Pete and I talked about other climbs we had been on, about climbs we still wanted to do. Since the time I had worked with Pete at the outdoor shop, he had set up a second career, a guiding service in Nepal. He was going there twice each year to lead trekkers and climbers on expeditions in the Himalayas. He tried to vary his routes each time, so that he could get to know new regions of Nepal, and his knowledge of the country and its people was rapidly growing. He had also unofficially adopted a Nepalese family and was helping them. He had made arrangements that would let their children go to school in Katmandu when they were ready. I told him I wanted to join him on a trip, but with the trekking seasons in Nepal being in April and September, it would be difficult for me to get away from my teaching job that long. This two-week trip to Aconcagua had really stretched the limits of what I could do during a school year. All of our other longer trips had happened during summer vacation.

I was enjoying the talks with Pete and getting to know Paul, Marshall, Jen, and Hal better. It was also good to be on a second expedition with Vernon, but it still pained me to be climbing

Aconcagua without Joe, with Terri and John at home in Denver. I wondered how they were doing and wished they were with us in Argentina.

By the time we reached Camp III, the temperatures were much lower. We still had clear skies, but found ourselves digging deeper in our backpacks for extra layers of clothing. We also found ourselves spending much more time gazing. The view out over the vast reaches of Argentina, and the views of other nearby peaks like La Mano and Mercedario were mesmerizing. In the evening, we watched the fading sun cast alpenglow across the peaks before the cold drove us inside our sleeping bags.

At each camp, we left some food and supplies that we would use on our way back down. Every item we left behind lightened our load, and by the time we were at Camp III, we had reduced our

We pitched our three tents at Camp IV at 20,600 feet on February 13, 2005, with plans of going to the summit the next morning. Photo by Steve Gardiner

volume enough that when we moved to Camp IV at 20,600 feet, we were able to make the move in one day. We crowded ourselves into three tents and settled in for an uncomfortable and restless night.

Chapter 15

February 14, 2005
To The Summit

On Valentine's Day, we got up at five. We could see our breath in front of us inside the tent as we bumped elbows and shoulders, trying to get inside the layers of shirts, pants, and socks we would need on our trek to the summit. It was a slow process, making way for each other and resting from the strain of doing anything at over 20,000 feet. We managed to eat and dress, and at seven, we left Camp IV.

The terrain there was easy walking, but the problem was the sun was behind the ridge, making an already chilly morning even colder. We hiked up toward an old stone shelter called the Independencia Hut where we rounded a corner and felt the sun on our faces. That was welcome, but by cresting the ridge, we also faced a strong wind coming up from the valley on the other side. With temperatures well below freezing, the wind stung our faces and made us glad for the thick down coats we were wearing.

We crossed the pass near the stone hut and headed toward a steep gulley called the Caneleta. Near the bottom of that gulley, we found a cliff and hid behind it out of the wind. We ate, drank, and made adjustments to clothing that might help us with the bitter cold. Out of the wind and with the sun shining on us, we felt warm and comfortable. It was a nice break from the chill we had faced all morning.

We started up the Caneleta and immediately felt the steepness. We were just over 22,000 feet at that point, so the altitude was definitely affecting our movements. We climbed slowly, but steadily, upward, using what Vernon called back-pressure breathing. We would fill our lungs with a deep breath, then push the air out with our mouths in a small o shape, making a whooshing sound. The pressure helps the oxygen reach all parts of the lungs to fight the thin air. The deep breathing in and out set a nice rhythm to match our steps. It worked well and seemed to make a difference. We stayed together as a group and moved efficiently.

Every step was an event. Every breath was measured, elongated. The altitude made us dull, slow. The morning cold gave us tight muscles, stiff joints, cold fingers, and mental resistance. It took away our upward drive, but we stayed with the battle. We lost any sense of time.

As we climbed above the windy saddle near the Independencia Hut, I noticed that the wind decreased. Halfway up the Caneleta, I felt warm for the first time, and relaxed. After two weeks of hiking and climbing, we were within a few hundred feet of the summit. I felt confident that we would make it and have plenty of time to get back to our tents in the afternoon. I tried to keep the excitement in control. I did not want to speed up. The climbing was too steep and the air too thin to move any faster. I just wanted to stay patient, enjoy the motion and the warmer temperature, and keep watching as the rocky ridgeline above, backed by a deep blue sky, became ever-closer.

I remembered the stories we had heard about the storm on the mountain just before we arrived. I remembered the man with the gauze bandages on his frostbitten hands. Our climb had been exceptional. We had made progress up the mountain every day. We did not have to wait out storms, and no one was injured or hurting. We were moving well as a team, and our summit day was a day all climbers dream about.

When we reached the ridgeline I had been watching the last hour, I looked to the left and could see Vernon standing beside a rock cairn. He was smiling. Behind him was a short rise, another ten or fifteen feet and beyond that, nothing. It was just after noon, and we had succeeded.

The summit had a metal cross on which previous climbers had draped beads and ribbons and other memorabilia. The ribbons were still. No wind. Clear skies. Warm sun. It was a moment of perfection.

Steve Gardiner, left, and Pete Shelley on the 22,837-foot summit of Aconcagua at 12:40 p.m. on February 14, 2005. Photo courtesy of Steve Gardiner

We took photos and walked around the flat summit area to see views from different points. We could see so far in the distance. The Andes Mountains spread out before us. Summit after summit.

We ate lunch, not even needing our gloves on. There were hugs and handshakes, as well as plenty of laughter.

The summit at 22,841 feet, was a personal altitude record for everyone on the team except Vernon and me. Vernon had been to the summit of Everest, and I had been to 25,500 feet on the North Ridge of Everest. While it was not an altitude record for me, it was the highest summit I had ever reached.

We spent a full hour there, a rare opportunity on a big mountain. When we left the summit, we started down the Caneleta, and three hundred feet below, we met another team coming up. They would soon reach the summit, and we exchanged congratulations with them, before descending the Caneleta, crossing the saddle near the Independencia Hut, and dropping down to our tents. Although we had only been gone from the tents for ten hours, it seemed like much longer. We settled into the uncomfortable, crowded tents for a second night. The mood was much happier now that we had reached the summit, so there was no complaining.

On the morning of February 15, we packed everything and started the long descent of the mountain. We took a short break at Camp III and added the items we had left there to our backpacks. Climbing up a mountain requires care to make sure that everyone acclimatizes sufficiently. It is a slow process, but works exceptionally well. On the other hand, going down requires no precautions other than maintaining good footing. As tired climbers descend, the additional oxygen is readily noticeable and appreciated. By the time we left Camp III, we realized that we were making good time and everyone felt healthy and strong. We discussed the idea of just pushing on all day and hiking all the way to Base Camp. No one wanted to stop, set up tents, and organize everything else, when we could go on, so the decision was made.

We stopped at Camp II and again at Camp I and picked up the food and equipment we had left behind. By then, our backpacks were very heavy. We just kept adding more to everyone's load, because no one wanted to climb back up the next day to retrieve anything. For eight hours we descended with the ever-increasing loads. Going down is faster because of gravity and denser oxygen, but the continual jarring on the legs is painful. By the time we reached Base Camp at 13,800 feet, we were exhausted, more tired than we had been on summit day. Or maybe it was the accumulated summit day and descent day, but Base Camp was very quiet that evening.

I had noticed on many trips in the past, that the return trip seemed faster than the outgoing trip. It was the same on Aconcagua, and of course, the argument could be made that on the mountain, the return trip is downhill. However, I had also noticed the same thing on hiking trips and canoeing trips.

Scientists at Kyoto University published a study in 2015 on the "return trip effect." They found this was a common perception and said it could be caused by a number of reasons, including that the way back seems familiar, so it goes faster. They also said that when we are going somewhere, we often have a specific time we need to be there, whereas on the way home, the arrival time is less crucial, so our attention is less focused.

It is also possible that the "return trip effect" only becomes apparent when we remember our trips and tell stories about them. Joseph Stromberg explained "that our brains appear to keep track of time using very distinct systems. One mathematically tracks the passage of time in the moment, with neurons that fire at specific rates and mechanisms that record how many times they've pulsed in a given period. Another, more language-based system looks back at previous events and tells stories about how long they took."

The next day, we rested and repacked our bags for the *arrieros* who arrived early on February 17. We had taken three days to hike the 30 miles into Base Camp, but wanted to hike out in two days, so we walked twenty-two miles to the Pampa de Las Leñas campsite. The weather was beautiful, so we did not set up tents, but spread our sleeping bags out under the stars.

Throughout the trip, we had talked with the *arrieros*. None of them spoke English, but several of our group spoke varying levels of Spanish, so we carried on in broken conversations and rough translations. They were happy that we had reached the summit, and told us they wanted to make us a celebration dinner. They started a fire, and when it was roaring, they placed an old bed spring over the fire and tossed on Argentinian steaks called *carne asada*. They pulled out fixings for salad and fruit. We feasted. After more than two weeks on the mountain, the fresh food was a delight. With our success on the mountain, the good food, and the friendly attitudes of the *arrieros*, it was not long before it was a lively scene in spite of the language barrier.

In talking with the *arrieros*, we discovered that several of them had been involved as support for the production crew which shot the movie *Seven Years in Tibet*. Even though author Heinrich Harrer's experiences were in Tibet, the movie had been shot in Argentina. They told stories of loading the cameras on mules to haul them up the valley to the movie sites. They talked about seeing the movie stars and working with the crews. They were obviously proud of their work on the movie.

I asked one *arriero* what his job had been, and he said in Spanish, "I was the second for Brad Pitt." Another round of laughter from everyone.

The next morning, we hiked the final eight miles back to the trailhead. We loaded our bags on the bus and drove a short distance down the road to visit the Cementario de los Andinistas (Mountain Climbers' Cemetery), a stark reminder that the massive mountains of the Andes are not always kind to those who visit them.

On the drive to Mendoza, we stopped at a vista along the road to look at a full view of the south face of Aconcagua. It is such a dominant mountain. I felt a sense of awe looking at it and had trouble thinking that only a few days earlier, we had been standing on the summit. It seemed too big, too imposing.

Back in Mendoza, we walked to the central plaza, the site of a fiesta to celebrate the harvest of the grapes. Mendoza is proud of its vineyards and wineries, so the grape celebration brought out everyone in the city. Music blared. People laughed and shouted. Children ran everywhere. After our days on the isolated slopes of Aconcagua, the crowds and noise were overwhelming.

We walked through the people, jostled side-to-side by the revelers. Becoming part of that moment, that tradition, was the perfect ending to our adventure in Argentina.

A Moment of Heat in Boston

_____
____

Chapter 16

The Road to Boston
April 19, 2004

As I passed the six-mile marker of the Boston Marathon, I felt sick, woozy, tired.

"Whoa," I thought to myself. "You have twenty miles to go. You better get control."

I slowed my pace, and at the water station, I took one cup of Gatorade to drink and one cup of water to pour over my head. I had never run so far in such heat.

It was Patriot's Day 2004. The Boston Marathon traditionally starts mid-day, and on this day, that meant a temperature of eighty-three degrees, the second hottest start temperature in the long history of the race. The day before had been a pleasant sixty-two degrees. On race day, the temperature spiked too high for running twenty-six miles. There had been warnings for runners to slow down, drink plenty of water, and be careful. Before the end of the day, the Boston emergency medical providers would set a one-day record for calls. Marathon staff and volunteers would be taxed from treating ailing runners and fans. Everyone was feeling the effects of the heat.

I tried to focus. I concentrated on my breathing. I relaxed and drank the full cup of Gatorade. I reminded myself that I had traveled all the way from Montana for this race, and I wanted to go home knowing the joy of running down Boylston Street where fans are often standing fifteen deep on the sidewalks. I wanted to hear their noise. I wanted to cross the finish line. I had to be careful. Run smart.

It had been a long road to Boston. I began distance running at the age of twenty-three, and after running a few dozen 5K and 10K road races, I decided, at age twenty-six, that I wanted to try a marathon. I entered the Black Hills Marathon scheduled for September 1, 1980.

Marathon training programs were not as well-developed at that time, but I found a program in *Runner's World* magazine, and decided I would use that. It forced me to increase my weekly running mileage significantly and include three runs of twenty miles or more. I stayed with the program and found myself feeling exhausted and questioning whether I had made the right decision.

I decided I would try to run the marathon in three hours, thirty minutes. That works out to almost exactly eight minutes per mile. Since I ran the shorter 5K and 10K races at a 7:00 or 6:30 pace, I felt like that was a reasonable goal to set.

I lived in Wyoming then, and I drove from my home to Rapid City, South Dakota. The next morning I went to the start line at Pactola Lake, twenty miles west of Rapid City in the beautiful Black Hills National Forest. It was dark and cool when we started running, and the fresh smell of the pine trees was inspiring.

I cruised through the first miles. I had rested well and hoped the exhaustion I had been feeling over the previous weeks was gone. However, by Mile 17, the tiredness was back in full force. I struggled to keep moving. By Mile 20, I was sure I was finished. I pushed myself, but I had no energy left. Each step seemed a challenge, but at Mile 23, I felt better. My stride eased, and my mind cleared. I concentrated on getting to the finish line near the Rushmore Plaza Civic Center.

When I crossed the finish line, I saw my time was 3:23. I was relieved. I promised myself I would never run another marathon.

That vow lasted twenty years.

Each year, more than 20,000 runners qualify to run the Boston Marathon. Transporting that many runners to the start line is a logistical problem. Each runner receives a ticket with a time to meet the bus at Boston Common for the ride to Hopkinton. My ticket was for 8:00 a.m, so I arrived at Hopkinton nearly three hours before the race start at 11:30 a.m. Buses of runners arrived continuously throughout the morning.

I joined the hundreds of runners spread across the football field at Hopkinton High School. Even sitting on the field, we were hot. Nerves were on edge. Talk centered on how to maintain hydration and keep control during the race.

I was deeply concerned. Being from Montana, I had trained through the winter and early spring. I had cut several runs short because of icy roads. Snowstorms and cold winds had plagued many of the early runs. Not one of my training runs topped forty degrees. At Hopkinton, under bright sun, I was sweating even before the warmup.

I moved around the field, talking with runners from across the nation and world. We compared training programs, nutrition ideas, and personal backgrounds. A shared goal makes strangers into quick friends.

When the announcer called us to the start line, I was talking with a man from Vermont. He looked at me and said, "Can you believe we are about to run the Boston Marathon?"

It was a strange feeling to come face-to-face with a dream.

I had vowed to never run a marathon again. That unraveled in June of 1999. Our family had gone to Helena, Montana, to run in the Governor's Cup, a race series that included a 5K, 10K, half-marathon, and marathon, with all of them sharing a single finish line. I had run the 10K race and was visiting with friends. As we talked, we watched other runners finishing their races. I saw several runners finish the marathon, a strong sense of accomplishment marked on their faces. A thought flashed in my mind. "Could I still do that? Could I run another marathon two decades after my first one?"

The thought left my mind as quickly as it had arrived. No. I could not. I remembered the pain of Mile 17 and the doubts and agony of Mile 21. I did not want to go there again.

However, the following September, at the Montana Marathon series in Billings, I entered the half-marathon event. After the gun fired, I found myself running next to Dennis Sulser, the principal of one of the high schools in Billings. I taught at another high school, so we knew each other through professional connections, but we had never run together. Since it was early in the race, we talked about how we were feeling and what we hoped to run in that day's race. At one point, he asked me if I had ever run a marathon. I told the story of my negative experience from years before.

"I have been thinking about running a marathon," he said. "If I did, I would want to be well-prepared. What if we ran this race next year and did the full marathon? Would you do that with me?"

"Sure," I said. I don't know if it was the excitement of being in the half-marathon at that moment, or if it was the question in my mind at the finish line in Helena a few months before, but I had said yes, and from that point on, I knew I would try another marathon.

During the next year, I toyed with the marathon idea. I could always call Dennis and back out. However, the curiosity was too great. The question of still being able to complete a marathon had been asked. I needed to know the answer.

I continued running almost every day. I had tried many different combinations for running and had found I liked planning a distance and pace for each run. I had one running friend to set times for running. He usually ran forty-five minutes which meant if he ran faster on a given day, he would need to run farther to meet his goal. That didn't work in my mind. I preferred to set a distance, and if I ran faster, it was a reward to be done earlier.

I found a new marathon training program in *Runner's World*. It was clear that marathon training had matured significantly in twenty years. The new program was much better. It included interval work on the track, tempo or pace runs, a long run each week which built up to doing three twenty-mile runs on alternate weekends in the two months before the race. We also read about a racing strategy developed by Olympic runner Jeff Galloway in which he recommended running a mile and then taking a one-minute walking break. This seemed to make sense because, as he explained, it allows a runner's heart rate to drop and gives a nice psychological break to an otherwise overwhelming task. Galloway learned that runners often ran faster overall times by taking these breaks, because they finished the last several miles at a steady pace instead of drifting off to slower and slower times, and most of them avoided "hitting the wall," an appropriate description for what I had experienced at Mile 21 in my first marathon. It would be easy to take these one-minute walk breaks while drinking water at each aid station. I decided to use the new training program and the Galloway method of walk breaks and shared those ideas with Dennis.

Our schedules at our schools did not let us train together, but on the morning of September 17, 2000, some twenty years and two weeks after my marathon in the Black Hills, we met at the start line west of Molt, Montana, and prepared to run into Billings. The temperature was fifty-four degrees, nearly perfect for a long distance run.

We agreed to run the first twenty miles together, to encourage each other and work through any rough spots either of us developed. After twenty miles, we would run together if we could, but each of us would then be responsible for getting himself to the finish line in Pioneer Park.

The plan worked perfectly. We ran each mile smoothly, keeping the breathing under control and taking a walking/drinking break every mile. Soon we had passed the ten-mile mark, then fifteen. At twenty miles, there is a hill that is not steep, but steadily climbs upward for more than half a mile. After twenty miles of pounding, my legs did not like the hill, but we started our walk break just a little early and walked the last bit of the hill, saving some energy. We passed the twenty-mile mark and felt fine, but at twenty-one miles, Dennis said he wanted to walk farther, and I should go on. That was what we had agreed at the start, but I still did not like leaving him. He assured me he would finish and would try to catch up to me later.

I remembered how badly I felt at twenty-one miles in my first marathon and was glad it was so much better this time. At twenty-three miles, I felt tired and slowed for a couple of minutes, but then felt better and ran well to the finish line. A few minutes later, Dennis was there, too, and we celebrated.

Our run at the Montana Marathon had been about finishing a marathon and having a good experience together. My question about whether I could still run a marathon at age forty-six had been answered. I hadn't worried much about my time, but when I checked my watch and saw it was 3:34, I was very pleased.

Another runner asked me if that time was good enough to qualify for the Boston Marathon. I had no idea. I had never checked the charts for Boston, because I believed it was for elite runners only. Since I wasn't in that category, I never expected to qualify for Boston.

I looked on the Boston Marathon's website and found out the qualifying time for a forty-six-year-old male was 3:25. I was nine minutes away from qualifying. For a moment, I was excited. Nine minutes? Surely I could find a way to cut nine minutes from a twenty-six-mile race.

Then I remembered how tired my legs had been, how spent I had felt after the race. That was close to my best at this age. Or was it?

Racing is doing a battle with the clock, fighting against time. I wasn't sure I wanted to take on that opponent again.

The following June I went back to Helena and the Governor's Cup series, this time for the marathon, and this time with a goal. I wanted to know how close I could come to the 3:25 I needed for the chance to run the Boston Marathon.

I used the same training program I had used for the Montana Marathon, including the Galloway walking breaks. However, I stepped up the intensity a little. Instead of three twenty-mile runs, I increased my mileage sooner and ran five twenty-mile runs. I expected that would make a difference.

Because I had a time goal for the Governor's Cup, and because I knew that doing math in my head would not be easy after eighteen miles of running, I took a black marker and wrote the mile split times on the inside of my forearm. That way I could just glance down at my arm at each mile marker and know if I was on track.

The race went well, and I felt good, but my finish time of 3:32 disappointed me. I had added two extra twenty-mile runs, nearly six hours of running time, and I had gained two minutes. I was now only seven minutes from qualifying for Boston, but I had no idea how I could ever cut that time. I needed to rethink my process.

Qualifying times for the Boston Marathon are based on two criteria—runner's race day age, and the average times of runners participating in the race in recent years. As average times change, race organizers adjust the chart to reflect those trends. For me, this was good news. I was still stinging from cutting only two minutes in the Governor's Cup Marathon when I read that the Boston Marathon Committee had changed the qualifying times in 2003 and added five minutes to my age group, the men's 45-49. That meant my 3:32 time was only two minutes off the new qualifying time of 3:30. There was hope.

That prompted me to read further into the details on the website, and I discovered the second aspect of qualifying time—it is based on race day age. The 2004 Boston Marathon would be held on April 19. I would turn fifty on April 17, and the men's 50-54 time, after the new adjustment, was 3:35. I could run the Montana Marathon in September at age forty-nine, and if I just repeated my earlier time, I would qualify for Boston.

That changed everything.

Until that moment, I never believed I could qualify for Boston, so I had been trying to get into the New York City Marathon. New York City reserves a few spots for world-class runners, but most runners get into the race through a lottery system. I had applied the past two years and been rejected both times. The rules for the New York City Marathon, at that time, stated that a runner who applied three consecutive years and was rejected was automatically given an acceptance for the following year, a provision that was discontinued in 2014. While I was still planning my training program based on the new qualifying times I had for Boston, I received my third consecutive rejection from the New York City Marathon and my notice of automatic acceptance for the following year. If my plan to run the Montana Marathon again and qualify for Boston worked as planned, I would be able to run the Boston Marathon in April and the New York City Marathon in November.

It would be a busy year.

During this time, I was the coach of our high school's cross country team, so throughout the summer, I had a lot of inspiration from running with athletes one-third my age. They knew my plans for the fall Montana Marathon and supported me. I cheered for them at cross country races during the fall, and in mid-September, they would have a chance to cheer for me.

My best chance to qualify for the Boston Marathon was at the Montana Marathon on September 21, 2003. My time of 3:34 from three years before would now be enough to get me to the Boston start line. Even though the Boston Marathon committee had added five minutes onto the qualifying time for my age group, I knew there were so many things that could go wrong in the course of running twenty-six miles. I trained well, covering seven-hundred-fifty miles using the same training program I had used for the previous two marathons. I decided I would also use the Galloway walk breaks. I was ready.

Several of the cross country team members were participating in the Montana Marathon as four-person relay teams. Each runner would run approximately six and a half miles, then hand off to the next runner. That would be a good workout for them, but I would only see them at the start. They would quickly leave me behind.

At the gun, I settled into my eight-minute-per-mile pace, which had now become standard and comfortable for me. I walked and drank a cup of water at each mile. I kept my pace steady, checking the time references marked on my forearm once again. I was keeping exactly on my plan. It felt good. I just wanted it to stay that way.

The hill at twenty miles had seemed daunting the first time I ran it. This time it seemed small, insignificant. I passed twenty-one miles where I had had so much pain in my first marathon and still felt strong. I checked the time markings on my arm and not only was I not slowing down, but I was actually getting ahead of my goal times. At Mile 24, it was very clear that, baring some massive breakdown, I was going to easily qualify for Boston. I wiped some tears from my eyes and concentrated on making sure I stayed relaxed and smooth.

When I turned the final corner and could see the high school stadium and track ahead, I was filled with joy. I had stayed strong every mile of the race and would finish well under my required time of 3:35. At that point, three boys from the cross country team joined me. After finishing their relay, they had jogged back out on the course to find me. We ran into the stadium together, and I finished the lap on the track.

3:25.

At age forty-nine, I had run only two minutes slower than my time at age twenty-six.

I was going to Boston.

Chapter 17

A Boston Birthday
April 19, 2004

After the announcer called us to the start line for the 108th running of the Boston Marathon, I shook hands with the runner from Vermont and wished him good luck. We both smiled.

In 2004, Boston still used one mass start (they changed to several wave starts in 2007). I was wearing race bib number 8618, based on my qualifying time in a field of 20,300 runners. That number positioned me nearly a quarter of a mile behind the start line. As far as I could see in front of me, runners were lined up on the street. Soon, those in front of me were walking, then jogging, then running. I never did hear the starter's pistol. I spent the next six minutes walking and jogging to reach the start line.

From the start, I was worried about the heat. I once again settled into my eight-minute pace and walked several strides at each mile marker. At Mile 6, I felt the dizziness set in and warned myself about the twenty miles left to go.

I had experienced dizziness from heat before. During the summer of 1995, my wife Peggy and I, along with our three daughters, had spent the summer in Chicago, courtesy of a National Endowment for the Humanities grant I had to attend the University of Chicago. In the middle of our stay, a week-long heat wave broiled the city. More than seven hundred people died, many afraid to leave windows and doors open because of crime. The buildings and streets of the city formed a heat island, absorbing heat during the day and releasing it into the city during the night. Humidity was high, leading to several days where the temperatures, as high as 106 F, created a heat index of 119 F. It was a terrible experience.

As I ran in the Boston Marathon, I tried to focus on staying calm. In fact, I had purposely created a distraction for myself. Earlier, when I discovered that my April 17 birthday and April 19 race day worked in my favor, I decided that the Boston Marathon was my birthday party. I typed a note on a sheet of paper that said:

Thanks
for coming
to my
50th
birthday
party.

I printed the note on 8.5 X 11 inch paper and laminated it. I used four safety pins to attach it to the back of my shirt, and throughout the race, I had dozens of people reach out to shake my hand and congratulate me. At least six different groups of runners sang Happy Birthday to me. One runner, in his early twenties, said, "Wow, I hope I can still do this when I turn fifty." Those moments were a great diversion for me, and I hope they helped the other runners as well.

Because my previous marathons had been in South Dakota and Montana, I was used to long stretches of road with no spectators. Not so at Boston. Cheering fans, even in the heat, lined the full marathon course. Fans handed runners cups of water and orange slices and sprayed water from hoses onto sweaty bodies. It was constant noise and entertainment.

I particularly remember hearing a roar ahead of me at Mile 13, the midway point of the race. As I got closer, the screaming of the Wellesley College girls grew louder and louder. At the college, I had to move to the left side of the road, because the decibel level was so high. It is an unforgettable experience to run through that section and see the signs, watch the faces, and hear the screaming.

At Wellesley, I concentrated to keep myself running steadily. The thought of the heat never left me, and even at the half-way point, I

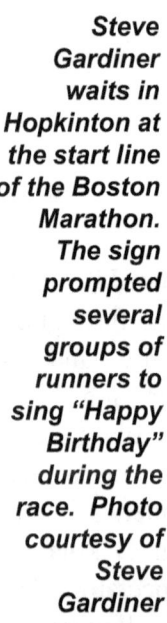

Steve Gardiner waits in Hopkinton at the start line of the Boston Marathon. The sign prompted several groups of runners to sing "Happy Birthday" during the race. Photo courtesy of Steve Gardiner

saw the signs of damage. Many runners were walking. Others were sitting on the curb, hoping to rest and resume. Some were looking for rides to their hotels.

No one runs the Boston Marathon without wondering about the fearsomely-named Heartbreak Hill. I had thought about it on training runs for months and wondered what it would be like to be twenty miles into the race and hit the rolling hills. Two smaller hills in Mile 20 preview Heartbreak Hill in Mile 21. Having trained in Montana, I did not see the hills as very big. However, after twenty miles of running, especially in this heat, they took a toll on me. Going up each hill did not bother me, but I noticed a change at the crest. Each time I started down, I felt a tightening in my hamstrings. It felt like the backs of both legs were being winched shorter and shorter with each step. By the time I ran up Heartbreak Hill, the third rise and fall, I was concerned about what might happen. Again I moved easily up the hill, but at the top, I felt the change, only this time it was much worse. I felt my right heel being drawn upwards towards my back. I hobbled to the right side of the road to get out of the way of other runners, extended my right foot in front of me on the ground, and leaned forward to stretch.

The aura of Heartbreak Hill draws the attention of not only runners, but spectators. Perhaps they want to cheer where it might do the most good. Perhaps they want to see runners crash and burn. No matter, the spectators on Heartbreak Hill are passionate and plentiful. As I bent forward to stretch, I could feel several people next to me move in closer.

"Get that cramp worked out, man," one said.

"You can do it," another assured me. "We're here for you."

"No way you are quitting at this point," yelled another. "Get back in there."

I stretched, feeling the cramps ease and dissolve. Like the one guy said, I wasn't quitting at this point. I also believed that if I had tried to quit, those fans would have thrown me back out onto the course. They were intense.

When I coached the high school cross country runners, I made sure we had two runs each week throughout the summer in the late afternoon. Heat conditioning we called it. I had not had the luxury of that training method this time. For me, and many others, the damage from racing in the heat was clear. Dozens of runners were lying down on the sides of the road. An occasional siren pierced the thick air. My usual eight-minute-per-mile pace was long gone. Every race to get to Boston was about time, but at Boston, in record heat, time did not exist. Only miles. As each one passed, I counted down in my mind. Three miles to go. Two miles to go.

In Mile 25, I looked ahead and could see another Boston Marathon landmark, the famous Citgo sign in Kenmore Square. For decades of marathoners, it has been a symbol of hope. The end is approaching. I believed I could finish, but I also knew that cramps could end my race at any point. I tried to maintain the delicate balance.

In Mile 26, we moved onto Boylston Street, the homestretch. I could feel deep emotion building in me. I would not be happy with my time, but I would be proud that I stayed with the challenge of qualifying for Boston, training in the Montana cold, racing in the Massachusetts heat, and finishing the Boston Marathon.

Boylston Street was like running in a packed stadium. Young kids were leaning out to high five runners going by. Everyone was yelling, even though the winners had passed by nearly two hours before. To see that those spectators had been cheering so long in the heat made me admire their endurance. I turned to a runner beside me and told him how excited I was to approach the finish. He never heard my words.

Ahead, I could see the banner across the street, marking the finish line. The grandstands in front of the Boston Public Library were filled. Fifty yards from the finish line I stopped. I wanted to gaze at it. Feel it. Remember the moment of knowing I was going to cross it a few seconds later.

I ran across the finish line, painted across Boylston Street. Cameras were flashing and people, runners and spectators alike, were cheering. A man handed me a bottle of water. Another handed me my finisher's medal. I felt the joy of having succeeded in reaching a goal in spite of unexpected obstacles. I shook hands with runners all along the street as we congratulated each other and shared an important moment in our lives.

I looked at Copley Square. I remember thinking it looked like a war zone. Every bench, every scrap of grass supported an exhausted runner. How eerie, in retrospect, that the phrase "war zone" came to mind. It foreshadowed the events of nine years later, when, on April 15, 2013, bombs shattered the sanctity of the Boston Marathon, a New England institution held on Patriot's Day, celebrating the battle of Lexington and Concord and the start of United States' independence.

Finishing the Boston Marathon was the first step in a hat trick of long distance runs for me in 2004. In June, I went to Dayton, Wyoming, for the Bighorn Mountain Trail Run, a 50-mile and 100-mile trail run through the beautiful Bighorn Mountains of northern Wyoming. I had no interest in the 100-mile run, but the 50-miler, a distance just short of two marathons back-to-back, interested me.

I got up at three a.m. and rode in the bus to the start. At six, the gun fired and I set out, hoping to finish in fifteen hours. The full race is on mountain trails and the constantly slanted footing took its toll on me. By Mile 28, I was hurting. My right knee was screaming from iliotibial band syndrome. I walked more and ran less, but found the pain was increasing. I stretched, but no improvement. By Mile 32, I was limping profoundly and vocalizing the pain. When I reached the check-in station at Mile 34, I gave my name and said, "I think I need...I think I need..." I could not say it.

"You need to drop out," said the man with the clipboard. I nodded.

Steve Gardiner paused to take this photo and enjoy the moment before he crossed the finish line during the 104th Boston Marathon on April 19, 2004. Photo by Steve Gardiner

"Don't think you are the first person that has dropped out today," he said, "or that you are the first to stop here with painful knees."

The aches and pains of distance running have a way of adding up over the years. Sore knees, tired feet, tight muscles take their toll, and one group I ran with referred to the accumulation as a "calendar problem." Too many calendars had gone by. We accepted that, rationalized our minor injuries, and went on with the next run.

Distance running is all about persistence and on November 7, I took advantage of my repeat applications to the lottery for the New York City Marathon. I initially had no intention of running these three races in one year, but with the automatic entry from the lottery, I could not pass up the chance and found myself at the start line on Staten Island.

We ran across the Verrazano-Narrows Bridge. The bridge has two layers and runners were edge to edge on both levels. With thousands of feet hitting the surface every second, the bridge vibrated. We made the gradual climb up to the middle of the bridge, then descended into Brooklyn where, a few blocks from the end of the bridge, the roads from the two levels of the bridge merged causing a jam of bodies. I realized immediately that the race was a spectacle for the city. Two million people come out to watch the New York City Marathon. They cook. They sing. They dance. They cheer. The sounds and sights and smells are a feast for the senses, and I was soon lost in the rhythm of running with thousands of other runners. In fact, I realized quickly that there would be little or no passing; I felt completely boxed in by the mass of runners for the first sixteen miles of the race.

We ran on through Queens and crossed into Manhattan before making a loop into the Bronx, finishing our sweep of running in all five boroughs of New York City. We crossed back into Manhattan and made our way to Central Park and the finish line, not far from the American Museum of Natural History. I met my wife Peggy and daughter Denby on the steps of the museum, and we walked back to our hotel.

My finish time for the Boston Marathon was 4:18, some fifty-three minutes slower than my qualifying time. I did not give that a second thought. I had finished. I walked past the frantic activity filling the medical tents, and on the far side of Copley Square, found Peggy. She had a dry shirt for me and several bottles of water. I drank as much as I could hold and put on the fresh shirt. We walked down Boylston Street to the subway station near Boston Public Garden. We would take the train to our hotel near Harvard Square.

My legs were tight, so the stairs down to the subway were difficult for me. I held the handrail with both hands and slowly worked my way downstairs. At one point, I felt sure that people behind me would be mad at my slow pace. I stopped and glanced back. All the way up the stairs were other marathoners, gripping the handrail with two hands and moving at the same pace.

Inside the subway station, the attendants had opened the gates to the trains. "The T loves marathoners," one shouted. "Today you all ride the T for free."

The train was crowded. I stood, crammed close to everyone else and drenched my shirt in sweat that would not stop. I felt dizzy again, swaying on the train. In the station at Harvard Square, I had to sit down on a bench for several minutes before climbing the stairs. At the hotel, I took a nap, then put on my Boston Marathon t-shirt, and got ready for dinner.

We had decided to try a small restaurant nearby that advertised the best hamburgers in Boston. When we walked in, I saw three other runners wearing their t-shirts. As we walked to our table, each of the other runners stopped me. "How was your race?" "Did you recover from the heat?" It was like we had known each other for years and had planned to meet for dinner.

A Moment of Terror in Tanzania

_____
_____

Chapter 18

The Roof of Africa
July 23, 2002

We left our 15,000-foot high camp at midnight, hiking under a full moon. We took one step after another up the long ridge that would lead us to the summit of Kilimanjaro, the highpoint of Africa. I was excited, eager for us to try to reach the summit. This date had been marked on my calendar for weeks, but I could have never imagined what an impact the day would have on my life.

Tanzanian law requires that Kilimanjaro climbers hire local guides, porters, and cooks, a system designed to provide jobs and income. Although we don't normally hire guides for our climbs, we followed the law and decided it would be fun having the guides and porters as part of our group. Our chief guide, Respicious Baitwa, came to our tents at eleven p.m. to wake us. It was chilly, but manageable, when we got up. We dressed and the cooks gave us tea and biscuits. We had food and water bottles inside our jackets to keep them from freezing and set off a few minutes after midnight.

As we had hoped, we had no wind and a full moon, so climbing without a light was easy. Respicious led and set a perfect pace. He said we would be steady with a few breaks, and that suited all of us.

When we were all standing together, Respicious jumped into the air and shouted, "We are ready to rock and roll," and our final ascent began.

The climb on Kilimanjaro was a reunion of sorts. Five of us, John

Jancik, president of ECHO Geophysical in Denver; medical doctor Terri Baker; Jim Schaefer, building maintenance supervisor in Milwaukee; Dr. Joe Sears, mass spectrometrist at Montana State University-Bozeman; and I had been together twice before on international expeditions. In 1996 we traveled to North Peary Land, Greenland, to make the first climbs in the H.H. Benedict Range and cross the sea ice of the Arctic Ocean to reach the northernmost land on earth. In 2001, we returned to North Peary Land, to traverse the peninsula, climb the highest peak in the region, and search for the northernmost mountain on earth.

David Baker, seismic analyst at ECHO Geophysical, had been with us in 2001 and joined us again in Africa. In addition, we had with us ECHO Geophysical's administrative assistant Nichol Schartau, Joe Sear's seventeen-year-old daughter Sammy Sears, and my fifteen-year-old daughter Romney Gardiner.

After we started moving, Romney said she was warm and comfortable. She had my insulated "fireman's pants" as she called them, capilene underwear, down jacket, and Gore-Tex jacket. I put insulated gaiters on her boots, so her feet were never cold.

We climbed easily in the moonlight. The trail was clear and each rock visible. We climbed for an hour in quiet. Only our breathing and boots scraping against the rocks broke the silence. At the first break, I told Romney she could not take off her mittens until we were sweating on the way back down the mountain. I got out water and food and helped her, and after only a five-minute break, we were chilled, and my hands frozen. Joe, Sammy, Romney, and I had agreed to stick together for the full summit day to support each other. The girls were climbing exceptionally well, and all eight of our group were together. Respicious stayed in front with the assistant guides, Valentine Kamugisha and Giriad Chagga, behind. Four others followed us from another group, and they seemed content to let Respicious set their pace as well.

At about 16,500 feet, I went through a twenty-minute phase of not feeling well. It had been ten years since I had been over 16,000 feet, and I wondered if this time might be when I couldn't make it. I didn't

From left, Joe Sears, John Jancik, Giriad Chagga, Steve Gardiner, and Romney Gardiner celebrate at sunrise on the summit of Mt. Kilimanjaro. Photo by Sammy Sears

say anything, but kept a steady pace and was able to walk through it.

The trail is well-used, so it is simple to follow and easy to walk. It is steep enough to give good progress but requires only minimal switchbacks. It is a good route. Starting at about 17,000 feet, Respecius, in his deep baritone voice, sang songs about the mountain, the plains, and life in Africa. His voice was so soothing and the Swahili songs so appropriate to where we were and what we were doing.

"Getting up in the middle of the night to leave was strange," said Romney. "We left at midnight. I was really energized. I remember Respicious singing, and I remember thinking about not knowing what was going to happen."

During the second break, Romney asked the elevation. I told her, and she quickly figured we had 1,600 feet left. She was warm and obviously feeling strong, as was Sammy.

Respicious, had used the phrase "strong like Spanish bull" several times, so at one point, he asked how we were doing, and I replied, "We are strong like Spanish bull. We are strong like Tanzanian *simba* (lion)."

After the break, we quickly resumed our hike. Respicious sang again and soon the full moon set behind the ridge from the Rebman Glacier. I expected to need lights then, but only Respicious used one. There was enough light from the moon to allow us to see. Our eyes adjusted, and we had no problems walking at all.

Above in the night, I could see a dark line. I assumed it was a bump on the ridge, because my altimeter read 18,300 feet. Nichol asked if we could rest at the top of the hill. No one really responded, but minutes later, we walked onto a flat area. Respicious announced, "You have arrived at Stella's Point" (where the trail first meets the crater rim). We cheered. With it still dark, no wind, and everyone feeling strong, we knew we could make it along the crater rim to the summit.

"I will never forget when we finally reached the crater rim, and I turned to Nichol and said that it felt like we could touch the stars from there," John recalled.

We drank and ate. Romney bit into a frozen Power Bar and thought she might have chipped a tooth. It was 10°F on Joe's thermometer, which was exactly what we had expected on our summit day.

We set out for Uhuru (which means freedom in Swahili), the highest point on Kilimanjaro, another six hundred vertical feet and one hour away. Our pace increased slightly, and the trail was wide and low angle. More and more daylight was hitting us, and we could tell that we would reach the summit just before sunrise.

The last fifteen minutes to the top, Romney walked ahead. She was excited. A dozen people were already on top when we arrived. We stood in amazement as over the next ten minutes we watched an African sunrise from the highest point on the continent. We exchanged hugs and handshakes. We snapped pictures. My camera seemed frozen. My hands quickly chilled. Ten degrees with a good wind seemed so bitterly cold after leaving summer in Montana. Romney was very cold, so after a few photos and a spectacular view of sunrise on the roof of Africa, we walked off the summit area and dropped behind the ridge that blocked the wind. Another climber stopped us. He looked exhausted and wanted food. I gave him an energy bar from inside my jacket, the only thing I had that was not frozen.

"The climb of Mt. Kilimanjaro was simply wonderful," John said. "Some of the incredible views of the mountain and surrounding terrain were truly awe-inspiring. Of course, summit night was very special under a full moon, as was seeing the sunrise from the top of Uhuru Peak."

With the sun up, we could see into the crater. We had read about the shrinking glaciers on top, and it was nice to finally see them. Romney and I picked up a couple of summit rocks and stuffed them in our pockets.

"On top, I remember thinking I can't believe I did this," Romney said. "I was so happy that I got to be there with my dad, John, and Joe. I was so glad I did not have to turn around. We climbed under a full moon with no headlamps, and saw the sunrise when we got there. It was chilly, so we spent only twenty minutes on top."

Those moments of sunrise beauty and happiness were wonderful. None of us, at the time, knew how quickly our joy was going to vanish.

As soon as Giriad reached the summit, he ran down past us to Stella's Point where he waited for us as we descended. He wanted to make sure we turned down the mountain at the right place.

With the sun up, it was much warmer. We left Stella's point about seven thirty and descended a different route, a gulley of loose scree which let us plunge step quickly, our boots sinking into the gravel with each lunging step. Giriad flew down the slope, and Romney stayed with him. We descended some 3,000 feet in one hour this way. We stopped twice to shed clothing and drink water. At the bottom of the gully, we found the trail over a small hill and into Barafu Camp. By ten, all eight of us were back in the high camp, and we enjoyed some food and drinks.

Respicious gave us until eleven thirty to rest. Then we would have lunch and descend a new trail, Mweka Alternative, to Rau Camp. It was too short a time to sleep, but we rested, packed bags, and had lunch.

The trail below Barafu Camp was steep and very dusty. We dropped several hundred feet, crossed a valley, and climbed a small ridge. On top of the ridge, we rested.

Beyond that, the trail was better. We had wonderful views of Kibo, the section of mountain that has the summit of Kilimanjaro, and the rough summits of Mawenzi, another mountain in the distance.

When we resumed hiking, Romney seemed to be struggling. After her excellent climbing through the night to reach the summit, she was having a difficult time walking and was going very slowly.

"I felt like I was having a heat stroke," Romney said. "I wanted to take off my jacket. It was cold, but I felt like I was on fire. I was so hot I had to rip my jacket off. I was lightheaded, foggy."

Not long after, she bent over on the trail and vomited. I encouraged her to drink some water and eat to keep her strength up. Jim gave her a handful of craisins, and she ate those. Soon, she vomited again.

Romney insisted that she had too much clothing on, so we pulled off layers. She was flushed. We drank more water, rested a few minutes, then moved on. I walked behind her and an hour later Respicious caught us. He had a bad headache. I gave him ibuprofen. Then Romney said her stomach was hurting and asked for Mylanta. John had the Mylanta bottle ahead, so I ran to catch him. I gave her the Mylanta, and we walked behind the others.

We soon fell well behind. I knew we were getting close to Rau Camp, our destination for the night. I wanted us to get there so Romney could rest, and I hoped, start to feel better. I took Romney's backpack and tied it to the outside of my own.

We walked slowly down the trail and found Giriad waiting for us. He had been so patient with all of us throughout the climb. We walked the last twenty minutes to camp, and I helped her get inside the tent. Terri, our team medical doctor, got in with her. Romney vomited two more times. Terri got her on medication, but it was clear something more serious was wrong. We ate a quick supper, but Romney was not doing any better. I thought we were looking at a three-hour hike the next day, but Respicious said it would be six hours. I was devastated. I did not think Romney would be able to hike for that long.

Terri and I talked at length about the illness. Climbers who get sick on a mountain usually have problems on the ascent. As the altitude gets higher, the oxygen gets thinner, and they feel worse, often stopping and turning around. In most cases then, they feel much better as soon as they descend. For Romney, this normal series of events seemed to be happening in reverse. I remembered her face in the half-light at Stella's Point on the crater rim. Her smile glowed as she told me how excited she was that we were going to make it. She was the first of our group to walk on to the summit. She felt strong, and it showed in her stride. Now, some ten thousand feet below the summit, when she should feel incredibly strong, she was staggering and vomiting. She looked frail and weak. Terri and I could find no reasoning in our mountaineering backgrounds for these symptoms. We were confused, frustrated that we could not solve the issue and help her feel better.

Terri stayed with Romney until three a.m. Romney asked for me, so I moved into the tent with her. We had only an hour or two of sleep the night before and now only about four or five hours this night. Romney couldn't sit still at all and was rocking back and forth complaining of "knives in my stomach." I rubbed her back endlessly as she complained of lower back pain. She could not find a comfortable spot.

The hours of that night could not have been longer. I doubted my decision to bring her on the climb. I doubted my role as a parent.

I had promised her we would get her off the mountain in the morning. At one point, she looked at me and said, "Dad, I am not a whiner." I knew that. It made the fear I felt even worse.

Chapter 19

The Trail to Kilimanjaro
July 15, 2002

It had been a long process to get our group to the summit of Mt. Kilimanjaro.

"I was really excited to go on the expedition to Africa," Romney said. "I was especially excited about going on the safari and seeing the African animals. It seemed so foreign to think about that. I was also excited to get invited on one of the climbing trips. I had heard about them for many years, so it was great to get to go. I don't remember being scared about going, just excited to go."

Part of our planning included Joe and Sammy driving from Bozeman to Billings, so we could all fly together. We met the rest of the team in the Minneapolis-St. Paul airport, and quickly noted that our gate was the same one we had used the year before on our way to Greenland.

From previous expeditions, we had learned to plan one day extra when we first landed in a country. It gave us a chance to recover from the flights, ask questions of the locals about our mountain destinations, and make sure that all our bags and equipment arrived.

At Kilimanjaro International Airport, it was my turn to come up short. My duffel with all my clothing and climbing equipment failed to show. I registered the bag, then we found our driver and van. As he took us to the Springlands Hotel, he frequently drove the van into the ditch on either side of the road because it was smoother in the ditch than on the road.

From the hotel, we could see the massive bulk of Kilimanjaro in the distance. There is nothing like seeing a huge mountain to put doubts into your carefully-planned agenda.

When we left Billings, the temperature had been 108 degrees, record-setting heat, so we joked about going to Africa to cool off.

On the morning of July 17, we sorted gear and had a briefing about the climb from Patience, who does an excellent job of running the show at Springlands. She walked us stage by stage through the climb and answered all of our questions. She arranged for a driver to take us downtown.

The driver pointed out a souvenir shop in the direction to the market. We looked through the shop and walked down the main street. Quickly two "guides" attached themselves to us. A few blocks later another one walked up and introduced himself as Thomas, an assistant guide on our climb. He said he had talked to Zainab, the owner of Zara, the tour agency organizing our climb, and she sent him down to us. He answered many of our questions and took us through the market to a restaurant.

"When we first got to Moshi, we were walking around the town and must have seemed a bit lost," Romney said. "A little boy came up and asked us if we needed help. I can't remember where he took us to but we offered to buy him a drink for the help he gave us. We went to a little store on the street, and we all ordered Cokes. He ordered something that none of us knew what it was, and it turned out to be a beer. He was like nine years old."

At the restaurant, the first two guides ask for tips and left us. Thomas walked us to the souvenir shop. Romney and I bought jewelry, wallhangings, statues. They would be fun memories when we got home.

Thomas walked us to the Zara office, but stopped a block short and asked for his tip. We suspected we had been scammed and wondered if he would show the next day.

Patience, who managed the Zara office, said a van would go to the airport to try to locate my missing bag. When the van returned, my bag was not with it. I was mentally making notes of what things I

Joe Sears, left, and chief guide Respicious Baitwa pause during the walk through the rainforest on July 18, 2002, the first day of the climb of Mt. Kilimanjaro. Photo by Steve Gardiner

could borrow from the other team members in order to go ahead and make the climb on Kilimanjaro. However, in the late afternoon, a second van returned from the airport with my bag. I was up late that night, organizing my equipment, happy to have all the things I needed for the climb.

On July 18, we loaded the Land Rover and drove to the Zara office where we met Respicious. He rode in a van with the porters while our team rode in a separate van. We drove out the highway and turned toward Machame. We drove through miles of banana and coffee plantations and arrived at Machame gate. We unloaded our bags, registered at the headquarters, and watched as Respicious walked along the gate and selected the extra porters he wanted for our team. They were all yelling, hoping to get picked for the job. After the porters were chosen, the loads were sorted for each porter.

We left soon after, led by Giriad with Valentine as sweeper. I walked with Valentine and talked with him about American education, computers, colleges, and his future plans. Giriad set an excellent *pole pole* (PO-lay, PO-lay which means slow and steady) pace, and we hiked through beautiful rain forest terrain. After two hours, we stopped for lunch - plastic bags of food that they had packed for us. We were careful to drink plenty of water. The beginning of the hike was at 5,900 feet, and we would end the day at 9,800 feet.

At lunch, Respicious caught up with us and talked to us about the day. We would camp near the end of the rainforest at the Machame Hut. Romney and Sammy hiked right behind Giriad. I stayed back behind Terri and talked with Respicious. He told of climbing Kilimanjaro once in thirty-one hours on the Maranga route and of another trip leading a party of eighty-four with fifty-five reaching Uhuru, the highest point. He said the ratio is three clients per guide and two porters per client. Eighty-four clients would require an army of support. Our team of nine had three guides, a cook, and eighteen porters.

We saw no animals, but heard several kinds of birds in the rainforest. We reached Machame Camp just before nightfall and found the tents were already set up, the mess tent up, and popcorn and tea waiting for us. Respicious brought jugs of water for us to pump, and I filtered water for him. He thanked me and instead of saying *karibu* which means "you're welcome" in Swahili, I said *kaburi* which means a grave. All the porters laughed loudly.

We slept poorly. Several parties were at the same camp, so it was very noisy all night. One of the worst parts was the latrine. It is an outhouse with no seat, merely a hole cut in the floor. I was happy, though, to see they had regulations for human waste and trash.

July 19

We were awakened at six thirty with tea and warm washing water. We packed a bag for the porters to carry, then our own bags. The porters dismantled camp while we ate scrambled eggs, sausage, cornflakes, toast and tea in the mess tent. They had carried nine folding chairs and two tables up the trail. We felt a little guilty about all that is being done for us, but what a wonderful way to go camping and climbing.

Giriad led us through the thinning remains of the rainforest, until we broke into the heather region. It had a drier, more open feel, and we got our first views of the ridges and vast expanses that make up the flanks of Kilimanjaro.

We stopped for a snack on top of a small knob and could see the porters lined on the trail both above and below us. An hour or so later, we crested a steep rise to see a flat area. In the center was our crew with tables and chairs set up. Spread on top was a lunch of bananas, bread, tomatoes, cucumbers, carrots and hot drinks. Too much comfort for those of us who had shared two expeditions to Greenland.

After lunch, we hiked out of the heather and into the moraine zone. The trail wound through blocks of lava, and it was amazing to watch the porters negotiate these tricky conditions. We could see the porters well above us on the trail and followed them over the large ridge until we descended briefly to Shira Hut. Again the tents were set, duffels deposited in front, and popcorn and tea were waiting. The wind was blowing hard, raising dust storms and spoiling an otherwise beautiful afternoon. We hid in our tents and rested.

Dinners were often potatoes, pasta, vegetables, bread, sometimes meat. The plates were large, and we never finished all the food. It often appeared in soup at lunch the next day, but we hoped the porters got their share.

I figured out which porter had my load. His name was Masanga Kinanda (his last name means bugle) and he wore pink wind pants. He was built like a collegiate wrestler. As they were loading, I walked over and helped him lift the load. He smiled.

July 20

From Shira Plateau, Kibo, the highest of the three massive peaks on Kilimanjaro, seemed an impossibly long distance away, but we knew the next campsite was at its base below the famous Breach

Wall which the renowned climber Reinhold Messner called the most dangerous wall he ever climbed.

For the first three hours, the trail was nearly flat with a slight continuous rise. We could see far ahead and behind as we walked through the high altitude desert. Lava stones lined the trail.

I walked all morning with Respicious who had been working hard to teach me Swahili. One of the first words we learned was *jambo* or hello. It is one of the finest greetings I have heard anywhere in the world. When we passed the porters with loads piled high on their heads, they always smiled broadly and said, "*Jambo.*" I learned new words every day and eventually we began short sentences. Respicious also explained how to change past, present, and future tense and to change the subject from I, you, he, they. That helped a lot.

We were above 12,000 feet and expected to reach 14,800 feet as our highpoint for the day. Giriad set the pace with Romney and Sammy always at his heels. David, Nichol, and Jim brought up the middle with Terri and John followed by Joe and me. Valentine walked at the back each morning until Respicious caught up. Respicious oversaw the dismantling of camp and load packing, then easily caught up to us. Sometimes Valentine walked with us longer, but then he usually moved on to the camp ahead to help the others set up. Joe and I stayed at the back, and I enjoyed tremendously the time talking with Respicious.

Respicious was thirty-one and ran the show on the mountain. It was clear he not only had the authority but had earned the respect of his whole team. Every day the system worked efficiently, effectively, and it only seemed that each day they tried to do even more for us. It was a finely-tuned machine. Respicious had a deep voice and hearty laugh. When he and the porters got going in Swahili, it was jubilant.

Valentine was twenty-three and so curious about the world. He asked one question after another followed by thoughtful pauses that brought up the next series of questions, always asked in a singsong voice.

Giriad was forty-seven. He was quieter than the other guides, but it may have been because his English was more limited. He was calm and friendly, and he set a steady pace on the mountain.

The porters were from Moshi, personally chosen by Respicious. He said they had worked together for a long time and many were his friends before they started working the mountain. They stayed together, and it was easy to see how much they liked each other and how much fun they had.

One very distinguishing feature on our route is Lava Tower, a reminder of Kilimanjaro's fiery past. It is a volcanic plug, formed when molten lava pushed through a vent and cooled, leaving the tower reaching for the African sky.

The trail forked below Lava Tower. The left fork went up to the tower and added three hundred feet of elevation in a close view of the unique feature. The lower trail was more direct. The porters set the lunch tables near the fork. We ate another feast, then voted to take the upper trail. We arrived at the tower, and I asked if it was okay to climb. Giriad said no, so I asked if it is not permitted. Respicious was vague for the only time on the trip, but a short while later, he stood up and said, "Let's go." We hadn't discussed it amongst ourselves, so when we left, it was Joe, Sammy, Romney, and me. The girls were giddy with excitement.

We found the trail and circled to the backside. We climbed two sections of easy rock and traversed back toward the trail. In twenty minutes, we were on the summit, and my altimeter read 15,100 feet. We shook hands, hugged, and learned that Respicious had never been up Lava Tower. Most groups simply walk by, so I shook his hand and said, "I'm glad we gave you a new experience in Africa." He was obviously excited as he was the first to yell down to Terri and Giriad who had started down the trail. Then he went to the other side and yelled down to the rest of the group resting below. We took photos and enjoyed a pleasant moment of success with our daughters and new friend.

We descended from 15,000 feet to 12,700 hundred feet at the Barranco Camp. The last segment is through a stand of giant senecio plants, an area called the Barranco Garden.

We enjoyed another evening of excellent food, and the satisfaction of a successful day on the mountain. Above us we could see the 1,000 feet of the Barranco Wall, the first step we would climb in the morning. The guides jokingly call it the Breakfast Trail.

July 21

In the morning, we set out on the Breakfast Trail. It was slow hiking, steep and the air was warm. After the flat section across the Shira Plateau, this felt like real climbing. Sammy and Romney loved climbing it. Watching the porters attack each section with full loads balanced on their heads was amazing. Because they must stay upright, they cannot use their hands and cannot turn their heads. They avoid striking the loads on overhanging rocks and at the same time must pass us to be in the Karanga Valley with the tents up by the time we get there. What a feat!

Joe videotaped several great scenes on this, and we all shot photos. At the top we rested. Respicious pulled out his cell phone again. By now the battery was low, so he dug in his pack and unfolded a solar battery, spread it on the rocks, and recharged the phone.

I brought packets of cream sours, and they were a hit. Each time we stopped, I gave them to the team, guides, and any porters nearby. In the morning before we left, we collected a sack of energy bars and other food. I asked Respicious if it was OK to give it to the porters, and he agreed. It was fun to watch them. They appreciated the gift and an unknown system of division quickly sorted out what belonged to whom.

After the Barranco Wall, we crossed other ridges to reach the next camp at Karanga Valley. From just past Lava Tower to Barranco and all the way to Karanga, we had spectacular and ever-changing views of the Breach Wall, Buttress Window, Hein Glacier, and other glaciers.

At the Karanga Camp, we filtered water directly from the stream, and took a walk up the valley toward Kilimanjaro. Jim, Sammy, Joe, Romney, and I stood talking at the base of the huge amphitheater filled with scree. On the way up, Jim discovered a cave in a slot canyon, so on the return, we explored that to a point where we found two beautiful waterfalls inside. Romney and I were up there first and had a nice talk inside the cave about the wonder of all the things we were doing and seeing.

The effects of acclimatizing were evident today. We were feeling strong and the hills went by easier. We were eating and sleeping well. It was a day of four hours hiking, so we all felt good.

July 22

I learned that *karanga* means peanut. *Barafu* means snow, though they use the same word for glacier and have no word for avalanche.

Five days of hiking with Respicius and his team of guides and porters had brought us to Barafu Camp at 15,100 feet elevation. This camp is higher than any water source, so our water supply for the summit day had come up on the loads with the porters. We had been amazed at the feats of strength and balance performed by the porters, but having them provide enough water for the summit climb at such high altitude seemed like asking the impossible. It was another day at the office for them.

We had to climb out of the Karanga Valley then turn left at the ridge to Barafu. It was another four-hour day, and I walked most of the way with Valentine and Respicious. I explained the Greenland trips to them and how Eskimos have many words for snow. I tried to explain dogsleds and how we use plastic sleds to haul our loads. They were astounded to hear we had climbed peaks no human had ever touched and got to name them. Respicious asked if I ever wanted to climb Everest and when I told him I had already tried, he asked many questions and told about one Kilimanjaro guide whose clients took him to Everest, and he became the first African to summit.

I asked him about tips, and he explained that some guides are crooked and only give part of the money to the porters. He said we should give the money to him, but tell the porters exactly how much each one earned. They really are friends and a solid team.

It was warm and sunny at Barafu. We lay on the rocks for an hour or so. Respicious exchanged addresses with Joe and me, and he wrote a list of Tanzanian music for me to buy.

We ate lunch, followed less than two hours later by early dinner. We packed our summit bags and by seven, we were in bed, anticipating the climb to the summit.

Chapter 20

The Long Carry
July 24, 2002

After the long night inside the tent with Romney at Rau Camp, I was glad when Respicious came to check on Romney at six o'clock. The park ranger was with him, and they were concerned. Respicious said we should move her immediately. I explained she could not walk. They found a wooden door from a hut at the camp and laid it on the ground. They put Romney inside her sleeping bag and then strapped her to the door. Four porters lifted the door and headed down the trail. I barely got my boots laced before we were off.

"The door was the most painful thing ever," Romney later said. "I was concerned about how I would stay on the door. They strapped me on. I felt like I was flopping everywhere. I was still throwing up on myself. It was the worst of both worlds. The door didn't work, so we left it. I could not believe how fast they were walking down the mountain."

It was obvious that the door was too wide and cumbersome. We walked one hundred fifty yards down the trail before Respicious stopped and asked if they could carry her piggyback. I agreed. Each one took a turn. Each carry lasted about ten minutes, then Respicious would call out the next name, and they switched. When Respicious carried her, he moved faster, and his carry was at least fifteen minutes.

The porters moved quickly, and I had to try to keep up which amazed me because Romney is five feet ten inches tall and most of the porters were about five feet six inches. At one stop, I took

Respicious's jacket and put it inside my backpack. Soon after, I strapped two porters' jackets to the outside of my pack. Carrying Romney on the uneven, muddy trail was strenuous work for them.

Joe had seen us quickly loading Romney onto the door. He said, "Romney didn't look good. I was hoping she just had a stomach bug or ate some bad food. We didn't think it was too much of a problem, at first, but then it started to look more serious. We didn't see her much at the camp, because she went straight to her tent and parked herself there. It was pretty scary the next morning, because we didn't know what to do. It was great when Respicious jumped in and picked the people he wanted to carry her down. They found that door off a shed or something and put her on the door to carry her.

"Sammy and I didn't know what to do. Should we go with Steve and Romney or stay with the others? I really wondered what was going on in Romney's head. We decided to stay with the others. We watched the porters leave, carrying Romney on the door. A little while later, we were all ready, so we started walking. Pretty soon we came on the door laying on the side of the trail, abandoned, and we wondered what had happened. Did they get tired of carrying the door? Did something go wrong? Are they just carrying her on their backs now? We didn't know. There was so much that was unknown. That was the hard part."

John had seen Romney leave camp on the door as well. He said he felt "Total shock and disbelief. How sick was she? Was it life threatening? I also felt badly for Terri and Steve. Terri, because she had limited medical supplies and tools to diagnose Romney's problem, and Steve, because of the feeling that every parent has when they see their child in so much pain and misery. The bottom line in my mind was how could such a wonderful experience go so wrong, so quickly for Romney?"

In just over an hour, we had descended almost two thousand feet and entered the rain forest. They switched carriers regularly, and at one point, one of the porters pulled out a blanket and made a sling for Romney to sit in. Each time Respicious carried her, it got a little longer.

I was so impressed. We were really covering ground. After two hours, Romney asked to walk. She walked about fifteen minutes even though it was deep mud. She slipped in her running shoes, but did a fine job, better than when she tried to walk to the bathroom in the morning.

In spite of the tenseness of the situation, I remember occasionally looking around at the beautiful rain forest and wishing I could go more slowly and appreciate it. More than once tears came to my eyes as I watched her bounce along on the porters' backs. Two more times she walked, and I had this odd feeling of unreality. I was running through a rainforest with five African porters carrying my daughter and no clue what was wrong with her. I wanted to be off the mountain, to be out of the situation. I wanted to see Romney smile and be healthy again.

At a rest break, one porter said, "*Ata fika.*" (She will make it.)

In the muddiest part of the rain forest, the trail was often stair-stepped with tree roots. With the number of boots that had walked on each one, many roots were greased with mud. One root created a spot where the trail dropped two feet on the downhill side. It was a difficult move, and the porter carrying Romney at that time slipped and dropped her. He slid down to the lower level, and she landed on her knees on the upper side of the root. She seemed unaware and later told me she had no memory of being dropped. Respicious didn't like that, and he had some sharp words for the porter. Respicious quickly took the blanket, strapped Romney to his back, and carried her through the worst section for at least thirty minutes at speeds I could just barely maintain. I knew my quads and soles of my feet would be hammered the next day.

John was also impressed with the porters. "I headed out of camp not long after Romney, Steve, and the porters left. The path down to the trailhead was a difficult one in places with mud that was ankle deep in some spots. I thought I was moving down the trail fairly quickly, but could not understand why I was not able to catch the porters and Romney. They were having to carry her down this muddy path, so they must be supermen at some level to move that quickly. When I got to the trailhead and found out that Romney and

Steve had already left for Moshi, my reaction was that the situation must be getting worse and all the joy of reaching the summit from the day before dissipated."

Respicious had used his cell phone to call ahead and a Jeep was on the way to meet us. When we got down to the road, we were exhausted. Little sleep. Fast moving on muddy trails. A full week of climbing behind us. Romney was glad to stop moving and lay down in the ditch beside the road. I cuddled up next to her and said, "I wanted to invite you on an adventure with me. I didn't mean for it to be this big of an adventure."

The driver was kind enough to four-wheel drive an extra mile up the trail to get us. When he reached us, we loaded Romney in the front seat. The porters (Emmanuel Muro, Godbless Mkonyi, Bungama Nyamuokya and one other that Respicious did not know) piled in back and tossed loads on top. At the gate, I signed us out and gave each porter a good tip. They were very happy. We got in the Jeep and headed for Moshi.

Romney was excited to be in a seat instead of piggyback. The run down had taken four hours instead of six. Without the porters, our group would have taken two or three days to get her down. It took another hour to reach Springlands Hotel. Patience met us at the car, and we went directly to the room. We had left Rau Camp at seven, and she was in bed at Springlands just after noon.

In the hotel room, Romney vomited again. I knew she was dehydrated, so I kept encouraging her to drink to replace the water she was losing. She did not feel better.

About three hours later, the others arrived from the mountain. I hugged Respicious and thanked him. I gave him the black Gore-Tex pants I had worn on Everest and the sleeping bag I used in Greenland. He was very happy. I also gave him several gloves, gaiters, and socks for Valentine and Giriad.

After Respicious and the others left us, I told John, Terri, and the rest of our group about the incredible performance I had witnessed. Those are five of the strongest guys I'll ever meet and for them to do what they did at that speed through the mud was incredible. I talked with Terri about Romney's condition. By then, Romney was sleeping soundly, so we let her sleep, hoping she would be better in the morning. I sat in a chair all night watching her.

July 25

Joe, Sammy, Nichol, David, and Jim left midmorning for the safari. We agreed to let Romney rest, then catch up with them in the Serengeti. Romney slept until noon, had a light lunch, and seem to be feeling better. John, Terri, and I sat at the table outside the rooms and talked while she slept off and on all afternoon.

She ate a good dinner with us and felt better. It was a quiet day. We were just hoping she would be well, and we could move on in the morning.

July 26

Throughout our travels in Africa, six team members had gone through bouts of vomiting and diarrhea, so we were now hoping that Romney had just had a stronger case of the traveler's bug and was moving it through her system. She felt better, so we loaded our travel bags, put the big bags in storage, and had James and his Jeep ready by eight thirty. We crawled in with Romney and me in back. She put her head in my lap. We drove five minutes, and she vomited all over the backseat.

We went straight back to Springlands and got a room for four. We put Romney to bed and sat out at the table again. It was sad to have all of us so close to the safaris, yet we couldn't go. Romney was really sad, because that was the part she wanted most. She apologized more than once for causing everyone to miss the safari. We still knew we could catch the others, so we weren't worried yet. By afternoon, Romney was much worse. Cipro had helped initially, but no more. We called a taxi to take us to the clinic. I was scared, but Terri said she would stay with her the whole way.

Chapter 21

Medical Mystery
July 26

The nurse took a blood sample and dried it on the slide with a hair blower. The malaria test showed negative, so Dr. Makupa suspected giardia, since there had been several cases recently. We went back to Springlands and put Romney on giardia medicine. She seemed to improve, so we got the idea to switch to hotels instead of camping. Romney liked that idea, so we repacked and made hotel reservations at Lake Manyara.

July 27

James had to leave with another group, so we got a new driver, Zahoro. We drove three hours to Lake Manyara without incident. Romney was tired, but not sick. Along the way, we passed several Masai villages and their herds of cattle. Twice we passed men on the edge of the road with their faces painted white. They were waiting for Jeeps of tourists to stop for photos.

We arrived at Lake Manyara National Park and while Zahoro was completing our registration, James came out with his group. He was so nice and said how much he wanted to be our guide. He said, "I told your guide to take care of my sister."

We spent two hours in the park with the roof of the Jeep up. We saw baboons, zebras, elephants, warthogs, guinea fowl, dik-diks, giraffes, impalas, water buffalo, and flamingos. At one point, a troop of baboons covered the road. One baby had just been born that day. Around one corner, we had to stop for a giraffe. We stayed until just moments before the sunset then drove up to our hotel on the cliff. The cliff itself is part of the Great Rift Valley and the site offers a great view of the National Park.

July 28

Romney had a rough night. She had stomach pain, vomited, had the twitching feeling in her legs, and slept very little. We told John and Terri to go to Ngorogoro Crater, and we stayed at Manyara. It was a long day, because she was so uncomfortable and also unpleasant to know we would not see our five friends at all. I tried to keep medicine in Romney, but she vomited several times. Two of the housekeeping staff brought her a hot water bottle which relaxed her and seemed to help. I gave her countless back rubs and could feel the sharpness of every bone in her back.

    I tried to get Romney to sit on the deck and admire the view of Lake Manyara, but she could not enjoy it. I tried reading aloud to her, but she couldn't pay attention. We tried going for walks, but she was too tired. She couldn't sleep, sit, lie, or walk. We both felt helpless.

    At six, John and Terri returned. Terri checked Romney but nothing seemed to be working. We would have to leave early to Moshi, and I hoped we could get her well for the flights. Again we were up through most of the night with back rubs, walks, vomiting, and medication.

    John and Terri were missing their time for safari in the Serengeti. I was thankful that they stayed with us. I needed their support.

    John said, "The focus of all our attention was on Romney, and that was the only thing that mattered. Nothing even came close to being as important as Romney's health. I have no regrets about missing the Serengeti."

July 29

We left Lake Manyara at nine. Romney rode well, but really struggled to keep her eyes open. We were at Springlands before one p.m.

and got a dayroom. Romney laid down on the bed and immediately vomited more of the thick green bile on the bed cover.

On the afternoon we were scheduled to fly home, Romney was very ill. We decided to go to Dr. Makupa again. He repeated the malaria test, and it was negative again. He also decided to put her on an IV. Again I was nervous, but Terri watched the whole process and approved. Romney had taken a full bottle of IV fluid but by then, Dr. Makupa felt she needed to go to the hospital. He recommended what he said was the best hospital in town, the Kilimanjaro Christian Medical Center. Our taxi driver took us there with one of Dr. Makupa's assistants guiding us.

We went to the admissions office, a room with three walls with a curtain. The doctor admitted her, but everything stopped until I went down to pay the fee. I went to the office, paid the fee, and brought the receipt back upstairs. Then he ordered an x-ray, so again I had to go pay a fee and bring back the receipt. Then he ordered an ultrasound, so one more trip to pay a fee and get a receipt. Each time I went to the office to pay, I passed a group singing Christian songs for inspiration.

The doctor on the ultrasound was from Minnesota. When he placed Romney on the ultrasound, he checked her very closely and found a bowel obstruction. He had Terri inside the room and explained his diagnosis to her. I was starting to feel better by now as everything seemed to be okay, though not quite the standard we are used to. With his explanation, I thought we were on the right track.

Romney was on a gurney, and a nurse took her to the elevator. We got on and went up. When we got off the elevator, any sense of security or well-being vanished. We passed rooms filled with rows of beds, four to six per room. The hallway was full, and they pushed Romney in behind a lady with a baby. Right next to us, another lady with the small boy knelt on a stool. She fed him a rice mix from a bowl, and he went to the bathroom in a bedpan. She would obviously sit on the stool all night with him. Her face and the faces of those around us will be etched in my memory forever

Through much of this time, I could not tell how aware Romney was of what was going on around her. Her eyes seemed heavy, and she seldom talked. Later, she told me she had a vague memory of being in the bed in the hallway. She remembered that the "sheets were yellow and there were people everywhere."

As we waited in the hallway, Romney's IV went empty. Terri asked to get a new bottle, but nothing happened, and Romney remained there for over an hour with no IV. While we waited, I could see a door on the opposite of a large room. The door opened several times, and the surgeon came out, his scrubs covered in blood. After a few minutes, he would go back into the room. He never changed clothes or cleaned up.

Earlier, a nurse had asked me to sign a stack of papers "in case we need to perform surgery." I refused to sign the paper and told her I would need to talk to the doctor first before I approved any form of surgery. As I stood there, my hands were shaking. I felt dizzy and nauseous. No scenes of rockfall in the mountains or close calls driving a car have ever been as frightening as standing in that hallway next to my semi-conscious daughter. I couldn't believe I had us in this situation, and I could only think that if I let the surgeon touch her, I wouldn't be able to live with myself.

Later, when I explained this moment to Joe, he said "the image of a Civil War surgeon pops into my head."

While I was talking to the nurse about the possible surgery, Terri went to the office to use the telephone to call John, who with Zainab, was searching for air evacuation. I didn't think it was possible, so I still assumed we would be dealing with the Moshi hospital. I could only look around in terror and imagine spending days there wondering if she would live and wondering what other diseases she, or we, might catch in the process.

I'm sure the patients had been lying on the same sheets for days and with the overcrowded conditions, it would be nearly impossible to clean the floors. Every few minutes someone screamed in pain, but no staff members moved.

The surgeon talked with Terri and explained what might happen. Terri kept demanding to get more IV fluid and to get the NG tube in place. Nothing happened. Finally they moved Romney out of the hall into an examining room and placed the tube. The process made her vomit several times. More of the green bile fluid. They got the tubing in--actually, Terri placed it--and the catheter and finally put on a new IV bottle. My stomach was churning the whole time.

Zainab called Terri three or four times and explained that she was making progress. One time she asked to speak to me. She explained that the Moshi hospital was okay for regular treatments, but she said do not let them do surgery. For surgery, we needed to go to the Nairobi Hospital. She apologized, but said the cost would be as much as $3,000. I said, "Okay, let's do it." She said she would look for a flight during the night.

John stayed at the hotel with Zainab throughout the process of trying to find a flight for us. Though I did not know it at the time, Zainab was going above and beyond to get us help. John explained, "Zainab was unbelievable. She was calm but very determined to make something happen. Zainab repeatedly asked me whether an option she was thinking about would be acceptable to us. Her calls to her sister discussing what could be done and how Flying Doctors could be arranged were spoken with an urgency that was very comforting to me. I just felt that if anyone could make something happen to help us get to a medical place more to Western standards, it was Zainab. We were very lucky and blessed to have her at the helm of that situation."

After the tubes were placed, they moved Romney into a room with three other beds. She seemed to be sleeping, but I could only imagine what was going through her mind as she saw the conditions and heard the discussions. She was so sick and tired that much of it, I expect, did not register.

Not long after we went to the room, Patience and Khaled arrived from Springlands with bowls of food. We decided we couldn't eat inside, so we went down to the parking lot for a feast. Patience brought a cell phone for Terri and that helped a lot. Within minutes, we had word that a flight would meet us at midnight. We packed up our things and walked Romney down. We met John and the driver

- the best one at Springlands, according to Zainab. I paid the final fee, and we left in a hurry.

We drove quickly through the darkened streets. Romney was doing well, and Terri held an IV bottle, but it quit working mid-trip. We arrived at the airport at 12:05 a.m.

It had been hard to get out of the hospital. I had to write a note saying we were leaving immediately and sign it. Dr. Makupa stopped me earlier and said, "These are the conditions under which we live. If you can't find transportation, you may have to accept this and have the surgery here." I heard him repeat this speech to Terri. The ultrasound doctor stopped by to see her and said, "Nairobi is a long way for her to travel, but she is not my patient."

We unloaded the bags from the van. The airport door was locked. As we stood there, we could hear a prop plane land and taxi. It had to be for us, but I had a sick feeling that something would go wrong so close to our departure. The van driver went searching for help and in minutes, the doors were open, and we were through. The airport guard ran us down to collect the exit tax.

Chapter 22

Safe in Nairobi
July 30, 2002

The airplane looked so beautiful - a white twin prop. The doctors loaded Romney and hooked her up to oxygen, medication, and a flashing heart and respiration monitor. She was very weak and slept throughout the process. John and I talked to the pilot. He was a Greek who lived in Florida, and flew Twin Otters in Sudan and was now "exploring Africa." He loaded the bays in back, and we were set. The doctor told us they arrange two flights per day and they often escort people home. The month before, he had gone to Phoenix and then Seattle twice.

"Incredible, professional, concerned, sympathetic, efficient and knowledgeable," said John about the Flying Doctors. "Simply put, they were everything we could hope for given the circumstances we were all in. If there was a more spectacular night than when we were flying over the summit of Kilimanjaro under an almost full moon, I can't think of one. The Kilimanjaro glaciers glistened from the reflecting moonlight which was stunning to see and distracted me for a moment from the situation at hand."

The flight was forty-five minutes, and we landed at Nairobi airport. We could see NW, KLM, and British Airways jets, a much bigger, busier airport. The ambulance met us and while we paid for visas, the crew loaded Romney and our gear and met us in front. It took fifteen minutes to reach the hospital.

All of this happened on the night we were scheduled to fly home to the United States. Because we had no way of contacting Joe,

Sammy, David, Nichol, and Jim, they went to the airport expecting to see us there. Obviously we did not show.

"After we got off Kilimanjaro, we went back to the hotel and prepared for the safari," Joe recalled. "We wondered if Romney could go on the safari. We didn't want to leave Steve and Romney behind. We had been doing everything as a group, so we hated to leave them. Every day on the safari, we expected they would catch up with us. We left the crater and hoped that they had just gone on to the Serengeti and would meet us there. Then it became obvious that they were not going to show up. It had been such a good trip on the mountain when we were all working together, and we wanted the same quality of trip on the safari. On the way back, we had vehicle problems and got back late. We didn't have much time to get ready to go to the airport, but we still did not know where Steve, Romney, John, and Terri were. We did not like that. Someone told us they had gone to the local clinic. It was heartwrenching to hear that. We flew to Amsterdam, and we went to the ticket agents to find out what we could do to help them get tickets to fly home later. We had then heard that they were flying to Nairobi, and the agent told us they could just get tickets in Nairobi to get home. We got on the plane to fly to the States, and I was worried about what I was going to tell Steve's wife Peggy. We decided we would say something about flight problems. We didn't want to lie, but we didn't know anything about what was going on with them. When we landed, it turned out that Peggy knew more than we did, and she told us the story. Hearing about what happened just tore me up inside."

Approaching a strange hospital in the middle of the night is horrid. I was so nervous. I could only hope we had done the right thing, that we hadn't moved from one bad hospital to another. They wheeled Romney in and the difference was immediate. This was a modern hospital, clean, well lit. What a relief! Terri and I hugged each other with joy.

"In some ways it seemed like an oasis of modern technology and westernized standards embedded in a world of poverty and Third World conditions," John observed. "When we walked into the hospital for the first time, I was tremendously relieved that we had probably arrived at a location that could most likely diagnose and treat Romney. From the limited time I was in Nairobi, everything I saw, and everyone I met further assured me that this was the place to make things right for Romney. To this day, I consider that hospital in Nairobi to be a tremendous blessing in helping Romney survive her deteriorating condition."

They put Romney in an exam room, and I went to pay the fees. Terri talked to Dr. Pankaj Jani, who was originally from India and had done his medical training in Miami and Chicago, and gave him the history. They sent Romney for x-rays while Terri and I talked more to Dr. Jani. By four thirty a.m., they were finished.

Though I didn't know it until the next day, the flying doctor had called Dr. Jani personally. He then went to the airport to get his car, then came back to get John, Terri, and our bags, and set them up at Silver Springs Hotel across the road from the hospital.

I also didn't know until the next day that Amina, Zainab's sister, who lives in Nairobi, had to go to the Wilson Airport to sign for the flight before they would leave Nairobi.

At five a.m., they moved Romney to her room. I had entered as a lodger, but no bed was available, so I slept in a chair with my head on the foot of Romney's bed. We were all exhausted after so many days of poor sleep.

At seven a.m., the phone rang. Amina was in the lobby, so I went down to meet her and thank her. She and Zainab had arranged a miracle.

When I went back to the room, a cot had appeared, so I was able to lay down and sleep. At nine, they woke us, and soon after, John and Terri arrived. At ten o'clock, we went for x-rays and tests that lasted until noon.

An hour later, Dr. Jani explained to Terri that Romney would need surgery. Soon after, he called me to explain. I signed the permissions form and felt surprisingly relaxed. I was comfortable with the hospital and doctor and finally something would help Romney. She was equally relaxed about it. I think that she knew something serious was going on, and she had been through so much from the porter carry, clinic, Jeep rides, and Moshi hospital that she was ready to let anything happen. She never complained.

At that point, I went to the hotel with John to call Peggy. There is a nine-hour time difference, so it was about three a.m. at home in Montana, and she had no idea we didn't board the plane in Tanzania. Neither did Joe and Sammy. I explained the situation and tried to reassure her the best I could by telling her I had as much faith in Dr. Jani as anyone at home. I am not sure how convincing I was during the brief phone call, but I tried to sound positive and strong.

At three p.m., the nurses came to get Romney. I watched as they prepped her. The surgery would take two hours. I'll never forget watching them wheel her down the hall.

While Romney was gone to surgery, John and Terri sat with me the whole time. I remember saying that parents often have visions of what their children are doing, but I couldn't bear to picture Romney then.

John and Terri were unbelievable. They missed the Serengeti without complaining and traveled to Nairobi without a word, insisting on helping. Without Terri to help with the doctors, this would have been beyond endurance, and John was incredible emotional support and so much help financially. I can never repay them for all they did for us.

At five thirty, Dr. Jani came to the room to report all had gone well. She had superior mesenteric artery syndrome, and the surgery is a gastrojejunostomy. Her stomach and duodenum were so distended that he expected the condition had existed for eight to ten years. It could have been exacerbated in Africa by altitude, stress, exertion, dehydration, weight-loss, G.I. infection, change of diet, and more. At six, Romney came in and was already awake. We talked some, then she slept. The nurses monitored her closely through the evening and night. Terri sat with her while John and I returned to the hotel to call Peggy to report the success. Peggy was relieved, but I could still sense how worried she was. It was understandable. I was with Romney and could see exactly what is going on. Peggy could only go by the reports.

Romney and I both slept eleven hours, although interrupted by nurses all night. It was the first full night of sleep for both of us in at least six nights. It was wonderful.

July 31

Romney was much better in the morning. We talked a long while. I told her how lucky we were, how everything had worked out so perfectly. She understood and said she could remember the Moshi hospital and some of the plane ride, but not the ambulance.

Dr. Jani stopped by. He explained it would take six to twelve months for her stomach to return to normal size. He drew a diagram of what happened during the surgery. He examined her organs and all were fine. After he left, Terri sat with Romney while John and I went to send emails to explain the details. Joe and Sammy were home by then, but Dr. Jani expected it would be ten days before we could fly home.

Romney slept off and on but was awake more than I expected. The nurses had her sit in a chair and then take several short walks in the hallway. She was very happy and said she felt much better. How could she not with the green bile no longer running from her mouth each time she laid down?

I was so happy. The relief of knowing she was okay - a feeling that seemed impossible on Monday - was strong after the surgery. It was one of the happiest feelings I have ever known.

August 1

I realized that Zainab had been so instrumental in saving Romney, but she now did not know what was going on, so I emailed her an update. After the details of the surgery, I wrote, "This has been an excellent trip and even with our difficulties, we have been amazed by Tanzania and especially the wonderful people we have met. You are one of those wonderful people."

Peggy emailed and wanted to know how Romney liked the climb. I told her that "the climb was incredible. It was such a wonderful cultural event as well as a major climb on a world-class peak. We had acclimatized well and summit day was a joy. Romney and Sammy really climbed well, and we made it from Barafu to the summit in six hours and watched an African sunrise. It was cold, so we didn't stay long, but one of the best things was that about 18,500 feet, we were still climbing under the full moon and Romney turned around and said, 'I'm getting really excited.' Eight of us made the summit, and we descended a scree slope to Barafu in about an hour and a half."

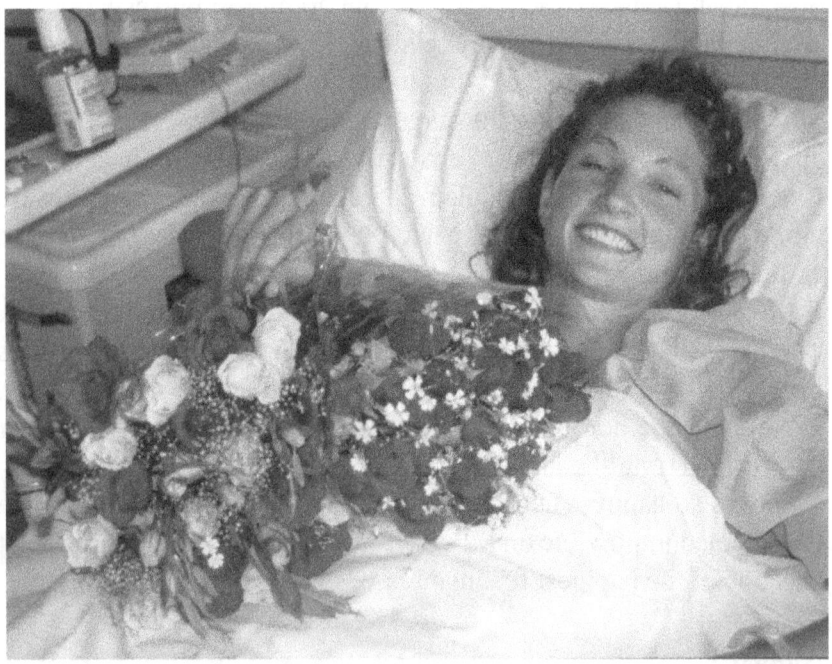

Following emergency surgery in Nairobi, Kenya, Romney Gardiner enjoys a bouquet of flowers and relief from her stomach pain.
Photo by Steve Gardiner

Then I added, "The anesthesiologist came in this morning. He explained that the surgery, which is called a gastrojejunostomy, is often used to bypass ulcers. It connects the small intestine directly to the stomach, but removes no parts at all. He said her extreme tiredness and drowsiness when we arrived here was a sign that her kidneys were beginning to shutdown.

"With the throat tube and catheter out this morning, she now has only the side drainage tube and her IV in. The drainage tube should come out in the next hour or two and the IV is in question at this time, but could come out even today. We hope to have her out of the hospital by Sunday. We then have to do the battle of trying to balance her recovery with available flights. We will hold the reservations for the following Sunday for a few days, but that seems about right for recovery and seat availability."

Later that day, Peggy wrote to me and said, "When I get up in the morning is when I usually have the emails ready for me to read. It is so strange to think of the two of you in the hospital so far from home, and I can't be there. Today the news has been sort of a jolt to me of how severe all this is – Romney really has been so weak and sick – I can't believe what you have been through, Steve, having to stand by and watch. Romney will have to tell me as I can't even imagine what she has been through.

"It doesn't matter when you get here. We will be so excited to see both of you and eager to take care of you here at home. I only wish it were sooner."

I responded, "Yes, this has been a difficult time to say the least. It was so frustrating to see her improve, only to lapse and fall deeper. It was ripping me apart, and I have to admit that Monday was the darkest day of my life. I am not sure I can ever tell you how I passed that night. The thing is, it has passed, and she is happy and well."

We were supposed to be in Africa sixteen days. By this point, it looked more like twenty-eight days before we would get home.

At four o'clock, John came over to visit. We talked for an hour, and then I walked him down to the parking lot. As the owner and president of ECHO Geophysical Corporation, he simply had to return home and run his business. Romney was safe now, but nonetheless, it was strange to say goodbye after so much time together. I hugged him and thanked him for everything.

August 2

Romney made fast progress. She got out of bed several times and in the afternoon, we went for a walk in the garden. She ate soup at lunch then a full meal in the evening. She was a day ahead of schedule. They removed the side tube and unhooked the IV, though they left the needle in. Everything progressed as planned or better. Dr. Jani mentioned perhaps getting out the next day.

Dr. Jani explained more details about the surgery and showed us her x-rays which I would take home. Her stomach was so grossly distended that it had pushed her intestines into her pelvis. The duodenum was over twice normal size. He estimated that her bowel functions had been abnormal a minimum of two years, but he expected with this surgery, she would function normally within days. Her scar was some six inches from her belly button upward. He said that in six months it would be a hairline. It looked to me like he did a very nice job of it, and Romney was pleased.

Dr. Jani said the small intestine passes through the middle of a fork in the artery. He believed that Romney was born with this fork being too narrow, and as a result of the expedition, she lost some of the fat in the pad that supports this fork. With it already narrow and already pinching the intestine for several years, the stress of the climb and travel caused the intestine to shut completely. With the bypass, it can never happen again.

We had both slept three full nights. I even went to the hotel and took a hot shower, my first in over a week.

Joe emailed saying, "We have been thinking about the two of you since we left for safari. We were all assuming that you, and Terri and John, would be joining us in a day or so. When we didn't meet you, we just assumed that you had modified your safari plans and that we would meet you back at Springlands before going to the airport for the flight home. Little did we know...."

"I am glad that Terri has been able to stay with you. It must be great comfort to have someone present who can advise you in regard to procedures that were being performed. Is she planning on staying the entire time until you come home? From the sounds of everything, the doctor in Nairobi has done a tremendous job, both in the medical treatment and in keeping you well informed of the procedures, preexisting situations, and recovery outcomes."

August 3

We waited all morning for Dr. Jani. Just before noon, he showed and said she could go. We packed our bags, and I rode with him to his office. He assured me again the payment was no problem. He checked the hospital bill and it was four thousand dollars. His bill was three thousand. I could cover those and the hotel bill, so I was glad of that. I collected all the receipts, so I could apply for a refund from our insurance company. John covered the flying doctor, so I knew I would need to get that receipt and then pay him back. Terri promised to write a letter to justify all the costs involved.

Chapter 23

Waiting to go home
August 3, 2002

We checked out of the hospital and moved across the road to the Silver Springs Hotel. Since Romney had been in the hospital for several days, we wanted to find something she could do that would be interesting for her, but not strenuous. We decided to go to the Ya Ya Center, a shopping mall about a five-minute drive away.

In the parking lot outside the hotel, we found a taxi driver, John Kinuthia, who took us there. He explained how he could take us on safari and to the Blixen Museum and other places. He left us at the shopping mall and agreed to come back to get us at five thirty. When we went outside, he was waiting for us. He gave me a business card which read "John the Baptist, Taxi and Safari." At the hotel, he outlined a great day for us for Sunday — four stops that would give us a good tour. He agreed to pick us up at eight.

As soon as John Jancik got home to Denver, he called Peggy to talk with her. She said, "He assured me that all is well. He did say for that for a few days Romney was way down and not doing well. He said that by the time he left he could already see Romney coming around and improving. I told him that we are all so grateful for everything that he and Terri have done for our daughter. Thank goodness for wonderful friends."

I responded and said, "You can tell from Romney's note that she is happy. It has been a long haul for her. We went to a nearby shopping center today. That was an easy walk with plenty of seating for rest. She enjoyed that. We are finding a few things to do for the next few days to pass time and build her strength. Her scar looks good, though still rough. He assures her that it will diminish in six months. He also told me that her stomach will return to normal size in six months to one year and that her other organs will move up into normal places.

"That's all for tonight. We are happy here. Everything has gone perfectly and your daughter is taken care of."

August 4

Sunday morning and it was raining. John the Baptist was waiting for us. We drove west through the district of Karen and saw the beautiful estates there. Private security trucks lined the road and John explained that the police won't respond, so the owners hire security.

We visited the Giraffe Center, and Romney really enjoyed feeding a giraffe from her hand. We then visited the Karen Blixen museum. She wrote under the pen name of Isak Dinesen and is the author of *Out of Africa*. The setting is idyllic. The huge front yard has old trees, tractors, and wagons. The house is filled with their furniture and photos of them hunting and farming. The brick building is beautiful and the grounds are so peaceful. The kitchen is a separate building behind. I had seen the movie of *Out of Africa* and noted the resemblance of the movie set to the real house. I decided I would read the book as soon as I got home.

We then visited Sheldricks where they take care of injured or abandoned baby elephants. By then Romney was getting tired, so we drove to Bomas of Kenya to eat lunch. We rested there, then walked to the models of the villages of the tribes. The houses were an excellent way of seeing their lives and John the Baptist explained them well. One of the highlights of Bomas of Kenya is music. Each of the tribes plays their drum music and demonstrates their dancing. It takes place in a circular theater, and we got seats front and center. The drums were excellent, and the dancers colorful and lively. Romney said it was one of the best performances she had ever seen.

August 5

Over the next few days, we met John the Baptist each morning, and he took us to see sites around Nairobi. We could see Romney getting stronger daily, but she usually got tired by the afternoon, so we watched how she was doing and went back to the hotel when she needed a rest. John the Baptist took us to the National Museum and through the city center to see the site of the US Embassy bombing and a host of other important sites around Nairobi. He also drove past a district of the city called Kibera, a slum area housing one million people. It was disconcerting to see the conditions, and Romney and I talked about remembering the view down the valley through Kibera, especially when a day has gone bad or things haven't worked the way we expected or hoped. A quick reflection on that view of Kibera would remind us that things could always be worse.

One day we went to the Sarit Center. We walked around the four floors of stores, then went to *ET, The movie*. Interesting that I saw it first when Peggy and I were teaching in Lima, Peru, and then I saw the remake in Nairobi. Another day, John the Baptist dropped us off at the Masai Market, an amazing market as lively and interesting as any I've ever seen. It could rival Otavalo in Ecuador. Near the end, I met a man who introduced himself as the "African Picasso." We bought a painting of a Masai warrior from him, and it hangs in our living room today. Not long after, Romney sat down to rest and a woman from the market was concerned. "Are you OK, sister?" she asked. It was time to take Romney back to the hotel.

It was also a time of getting caught up with friends who had been separated by the nature of the events that happened on our scheduled departure date. Joe sent a note saying "It is really good to hear that Romney is doing well. It has been hard on this end, thinking about all of you and being essentially helpless to provide any sort of assistance. This is not how I would have liked to leave our teammates. Our flights back home were uneventful, just long. It was thirty-three hours from the time we left KIA to the time we pulled into the driveway. We had dinner with Peggy last Tuesday evening before we continued on to Bozeman. This was where we first found out that you had all flown to Nairobi and that Romney had surgery. It was a real shock to Sammy and me."

He also wrote to John and Terri. "I would like to thank you for all that you and Terri have done for Steve and Romney. It is a real tribute to, and remarkable demonstration of human compassion. I can't thank you enough. You have put in a tremendous amount of time and most likely financial effort to their cause. It is bad that something like this had to happen, but it is great to know that there are two great people like you and Terri who were on the scene. I think that it was a shock to all of us that returned from the safari to learn that Romney had been hospitalized. I know that Sammy and I both felt helpless during all of this. I feel like I should have been there with them, doing something to help out and make the situation better. It is too bad that we were in such a rush to get to the airport a week ago. Everything seemed so scattered in my mind."

August 7

Dr. Jani examined Romney and removed the stitches. All was well. He explained that he couldn't make a second attachment to the duodenum because it was so swollen. He said her stomach would soon grow used to the bile and function normally. He gave her a prescription which we filled downstairs.

"I don't ever remember feeling sick before Africa," Romney recalled. "I am sure Dr. Jani is right in saying that I probably don't know what it feels like to have a normal stomach, but I guess I don't know what I am missing. I don't remember having stomach pains or issues before the surgery, so my pre-surgery stomach is my version of what a normal stomach feels like."

August 8

Romney's birthday was August 9. She was excited to turn sixteen. I told her she had to wait until nine a.m. Nairobi time to turn sixteen because she was born in Mountain Time, but she said she would count it at midnight in Nairobi. John the Baptist planned to take us on safari for the birthday girl.

August 9

At eight, I went to Dr. Jani's office to pay the bill, but they don't accept credit cards. Dr. Jani gave me the x-rays, report, and bill. He said he didn't want me to go get cash, because it would cost too much, so he wanted me to send him a bank check. How trusting! I got his email address, so I could report on Romney and let him know when the check was mailed.

We had looked forward to Romney's birthday all week and had saved the safari to Nairobi National Park as a treat for her. It was. We were able to drive from ten thirty until five thirty in the park and Romney was strong the whole time. We saw giraffes, zebras, gazelles, warthogs, water buffalo, guinea fowl, ostrich, vultures, crocodiles, and a rhino. The rhino was at forty yards, and we could hear it eating the stocks of grass. Nearby we also got within ten yards of zebra. We had great views of zebra, giraffe, and gazelle together. It was exactly the kind of day we needed to finish the trip perfectly and positively.

August 10

I emailed Peggy to say, "This should be our last letter from Africa. If all goes well, we leave for the airport in two hours. We are all ready. We have a four-hour layover in Amsterdam and another four hours in Minneapolis, so we should have no problem making connections. We look forward to seeing you at six o'clock Sunday evening.

"We walked around the city center today and had a good walk. I think Romney looks better. Her back is still sore which Dr. Jani says is a normal response to major surgery. Her scar has really healed nicely. It looks so much better now that she said we should have taken a picture of it the day after surgery."

We boarded our plane to travel home, and I was anxious. I wanted Romney to be comfortable and relaxed for the flights. I hoped it would not be a difficult, painful experience. She had already been through enough.

Our first flight landed in Amsterdam, and we were lined up to talk with security officials. The man assigned to us asked questions. "Do you have any items that use batteries?" I told him about our cameras. "Have you ever loaned these items to anyone?"

I wondered if our one-way tickets from Africa to the United States would set off a warning, and obviously, they had. He asked question after question, and I could see Romney starting to fade. "Why are you traveling on one-way tickets from Africa," he finally asked. I explained the surgery, and he looked doubtful. Romney had been quiet until this point, but she had had enough. When he doubted the surgery, she stepped toward him and lifted up her shirt. The angry, purple scar was right in front of him. He quickly handed us our papers and moved us through the line. End of the questions.

Romney was strong throughout the flights, and when we got home, she soon learned that the African experience was powerful. Over the years, she got good mileage out of it in speeches and papers on topics like "What is one thing about you that makes you unique?" She said, "It is a good ice breaker. I wrote about it several times in college."

In Greenland, it had been a thousand miles to the nearest village, so our memories there were of untouched glaciers, deep crevasses, unclimbed peaks, and silent vistas. While Kilimanjaro is beautiful and the animals of the safaris fascinating, my memories of Africa will be faces — Respicius and the porters helping us climb the mountain and carrying Romney down, the jeep drivers who transported us, the pilot and doctors on the emergency flight, the nurses and doctors at Nairobi Hospital, and John and Terri who sacrificed their time and energy to help Romney and me when we needed it. Expeditions are designed for adventure, and this time we got more than our share. Although it was at times frightening, we are left with wonderful memories of the mountain and safari, of the African people and our own close friends.

August 25

When we got home, I needed to talk to the rest of the team. I emailed and said, "I am sorry that things worked out in such confusion at the end and we did not get to say goodbye to many of our teammates, but I couldn't control the timing of the events. Romney and I are both disappointed that we missed the handing out of T-shirts to the porters and the singing of the Kilimanjaro song. We wanted to be involved in all of that, and of course, we are sad to have missed the Serengeti and the many enjoyable times we would have had together there. We are very happy the way things worked out."

I included a brief summary of the events that happened after our team split apart.

I also wanted to write a thank John and Terri who had done so much for us. I wrote, "What a summer is has been! I have dreamed of climbing Kilimanjaro and going on an African safari for some fifteen years. Because of the generous offer you made this year, I got to share that dream with some very wonderful people. I can never thank you enough for providing the funding for nine of us to visit Africa and see the wonders of that continent. I know everyone involved was impressed by what we saw, and we now have great friends in Tanzania that will provide memories for a lifetime. It is unbelievable that we were able to get five of the original Greenland team members back together again for an African expedition. Just think where that group of people has been and the amazing things we have seen together. Without the financial marketing and personal financial support that you two have provided, none of those expeditions would have ever happened. I will never be able to thank you enough for that support.

"Then, when things seemed so incredible, I was faced with perhaps the most difficult situation of my life. I will never forget how badly I felt when the two of you backed off the safari to stay with Romney and me at Springlands. Romney was so disappointed in not getting to go, because that was the part she wanted most, and I know all of us were equally disappointed, but the situation just wasn't right. To be so far from home and have good friends there to help is truly a gift. Then, with the later developments, I don't know how I could have ever handled that night at the hospital. Without you there to watch each step, Terri, I would have gone crazy. And without you, John, on the phone with Zainab, the emergency flight would have never happened. When I think back on all that happened, it is an incredible series of events which all worked out exactly right. It worked out right because both of you used your talents and skills to the maximum and provided critical help at exactly the moment it was needed. Romney and I will be forever grateful.

"I know Terri stayed much longer in Africa than she ever planned, but I hope that the fun we had in Nairobi after the danger had passed was compensation for being away from home for so long.

"Thank you both so much. Difficult times help put things into perspective, and this trip certainly did that. I learned a lot about myself, my daughter, and my close friends. While Kilimanjaro was a wonderful climb, and the animals were all I hoped, the lasting memory of this trip is of friends. Thank you."

A month later, I realized that I needed to let Dr. Jani know how Romney was doing. I told him about her progress and thanked him and the nurses at Nairobi Hospital. He responded, "I am glad to note that your daughter has fully recovered and has fond memories of our country."

Terri wrote a letter explaining the medical situation for Romney and justifying the flight to Nairobi. I was able to organize the bills from the hospitals and doctors and filed an insurance claim. In the end, everything was reimbursed except the stay in the hotel.

But the influence of our travels in Africa did not end when we got home. Two years after we returned, I received a call from Bishop Eliudi Issangya from Tanzania. He was in Montana fundraising for his church and school and called me. He had heard from others about Romney's experience and told me that his son had been injured at the same time and ended up in the same two hospitals we had been in. He, too, felt the first hospital in Moshi was frightening and had decided to start an effort to build a new hospital there, the New Hope International Hospital in Sakila, Tanzania. He asked if I would help him.

As a high school English teacher, there wasn't much I could do to help with finances or medical supplies/support, but I teamed up with four other groups in Billings who were doing projects to help African communities in Tanzania, Uganda, and Rwanda with water projects for clinics, schools, and churches. The five projects came together under the broad banner of the international World Water Day and locally through the efforts of Hope 2 One Life (H2O). The emphasis is on an awareness of the world water crisis and the importance of clean water in medical care, education, and life throughout the world.

The international event for World Water Day is held each March, so we set out to organize a Walk for Water on the campus of Montana State University—Billings, and set up demonstrations of bio-sand filters, Life Straws, water carrying stations, and information booths for each of the African humanitarian projects. Over three hundred people attended that first World Water Day, so we continued organizing them, eventually moving our walk to the campus of Rocky Mountain College. Participating in nine annual events, I was able to send a check to Bishop Issangya's hospital project every year. Other organizations have been able to drill water wells in Uganda and provide health services and health education to many villages.

The framework of the New Hope International Hospital has been constructed. Building progress is slow in Tanzania, so the New Hope organization created the Sakila Clinic to meet the immediate needs of the people. Lines form outside the clinic each day as community members seek medical care and have their needs met. After four years, the Clinic was upgraded to a Dispensary and now has a full-time doctor and several full-time nurses. One day, a modern hospital will take care of more serious concerns that affect the lives of thousands of people living near the base of Mt. Kilimanjaro.

A Moment of Solitude
in the Beartooth Mountains

———————
————

Chapter 24

Alone Near Lonesome Mountain
August 10, 2001

Three days to hike alone in the Beartooth Mountains of Montana.

Delicious.

I love the feeling of setting out into the mountains on my own. It is a chance to savor the quiet, to think, to enjoy the rivers, lakes, and peaks. It is time to wander and wonder.

Alone, I have no need to hurry or meet any expectations. I can walk when I want, stop when I need, all without discussing it with anyone else. Camping solo is a treat. No one to wait for, no one to worry about. It is a joy to be moving, taking care of myself.

With that freedom, however, comes the fact there I can't get a second opinion about a route decision or a judgment on weather conditions. I have to make my choices and then live with the consequences. Hiking alone means I have to carry everything and do everything. No splitting loads or chores with a partner. It also means that if anything goes wrong, there is no backup. No one will help me. With three decades of hiking and climbing experience, I feel confident in myself in the wilderness, but accidents can happen. I keep that in mind always.

I drove up the switchbacks on the spectacular Beartooth Highway and arrived at the Clay Butte trailhead, some twenty-three miles east of Cooke City, to hike the Green Lake Loop. Most hiking trips ascend from the trailhead to the lakes and peaks above, but Clay Butte is a rare instance of the trailhead being higher elevation than most of the hike. The Beartooth Highway crosses the Beartooth Plateau, a unique mountaintop area spotted with hundreds of pristine lakes. A network of trails gives access to these lakes, and from the Clay Butte trailhead, I could look out across the vast expanse of the Absaroka-Beartooth Wilderness Area and see where I would be hiking for the next three days.

I hiked past Native Lake and Box Lake and paused for lunch at Mule Lake. It felt so good to be walking from lake to lake. Thin clouds were forming in the west, but for the most part, the day was pleasant. I was four miles into my hike and had not seen anyone else.

After lunch at Mule Lake, I returned to the trail and could see Thiel Lake through the trees to my left. Just beyond, I climbed up the steep trail heading toward Martin Lake Basin. My pack weighed thirty-five pounds, so I took shorter strides, used my trekking poles, and slowed my pace. Riding an ATV or a mountain bike is exciting and fun, but the scenery moves by too quickly. Fortunately, vehicles and bikes are not allowed in wilderness areas, because wilderness should be seen at a more leisurely pace. For a hiker, terrain dictates speed, and a hill like the one near Thiel Lake gives plenty of time to appreciate beauty. As one hiking partner often told me, "I am not tired. I'm just pausing to admire the scenery."

Near the top of the steep section above Thiel Lake, I met a family of three. We simply said hello, smiled, and passed on the trail, respecting each other's privacy. I finished climbing up the steep section, and not long after, began descending into the basin holding the four lakes I wanted to see, one of which would be my home for the night. As I hiked down, I could see Wright and Martin lakes.

Gorgeous.

Granite and green.

After six miles of hiking, I reached the shore of Wright Lake. I dropped my pack on a soft, grassy area and walked along the water's edge, looking full circle. Just what I hoped. No one else was there. I would have Wright Lake to myself that night.

One second. A brief glimpse in my headlights. A moose in the road.

I slammed on my brakes as the moose darted to the left. I reached it just as it hit mid-stride. Its rear hooves raised in the air and clicked against my front bumper as I skidded past. No harm to my car, no harm to the moose, but enough adrenaline to fuel a full day of climbing.

I was on the highway just north of Red Lodge, Montana, on a section of road lined on both sides with tall trees, when I saw the moose. It was long before daylight, and the trees formed a blackened tunnel, hiding the dark moose until the last instant.

I had wanted to leave the trailhead to climb Lonesome Mountain at daylight, so I left my home in Billings at four a.m. and drove up Beartooth Pass beyond Long Lake and Little Bear Lake to the trailhead at Island Lake. This trail, which passes Night Lake and several unnamed lakes, is relatively flat, easy, and makes for good early-morning walking. I hiked past the north end of Beauty Lake, continually looking to the north for glimpses of the summit of Lonesome Mountain. When I had a good view of my goal for the day, I left the trail, turned to the north, and traveled cross country up the valley to the base of Lonesome Mountain.

I sat on a flat boulder, ate a granola bar for my second breakfast, and selected a route up the southwest corner of Lonesome Mountain. Rested, I set out to find a way through the jumble of boulders and small cliffs that cover the mountainside.

I had climbed Lonesome Mountain ten years before with a friend, but this time I was climbing alone. From the earlier climb, I remembered how beautiful the scenery was, and this time I wanted to experience it with no one else around. I don't climb by myself very often, and never where the terrain would warrant a rope and protection, but sometimes I appreciate being outdoors hiking on a trail with only my own thoughts for company.

By eleven, I scrambled over a small cliff band and walked onto the summit of Lonesome Mountain. The summit is the central point, the hub, where the spokes of three glacial valleys meet. By turning full circle, I could look out over dozens of other peaks and look into the heart of each of those valleys. The beautiful lakes that are one of the chief characteristics of the Beartooth Mountains glistened in the mid-day sun. I counted forty lakes visible from that one spot. I've been on a lot of summits in my years of climbing, but I can't remember another spot where I could stand and look at forty lakes at one time.

I sat on a warm, slanting boulder, ate my lunch, and enjoyed the summer sun. Every few minutes, I shifted a few degrees to the right, so that as I ate my lunch, I had a view much like that of the patrons in a revolving restaurant whose view gradually changes as they eat their meals.

Rather than descend the same route I climbed, I decided to go down the east side of Lonesome Mountain to Albino Lake and hike past Becker Lake to meet the trail I had taken in the early morning. The miles of hiking and climbing, the beautiful scenery from the summit, and the peaceful feeling created by being alone in the wilderness had helped me overcome the fear and adrenaline I had experienced a dozen hours earlier when I encountered the moose on the highway.

After arriving in the Martin Lake Basin, I set up camp at Wright Lake. Traveling unaccompanied meant I had to do it all—pitch the tent, cook dinner, clean up. It also meant a perfectly quiet evening beside a mountain lake.

No worries. Silent peace.

I tried to do solo day hikes or an overnight camping trip at least once a summer for several years. I especially liked taking a retreat like this in late August, just before I needed to return to my classroom and teach high school English. I did these solo trips for years, knowing that I returned from each of these personal trips renewed, clean. I didn't understand the full value of these trips until 2012 when I read Susan Cain's book *Quiet*. She examines the difference between introvert and extrovert personalities. She writes, "Introverts recharge their batteries by being alone; extroverts need to recharge when they don't socialize enough."

Working as I did in a building with two thousand people, I often felt drained at the end of the day. It was not that the work was physically demanding, although it could be, but as an introvert in an extrovert world, I felt the need, as Cain explained, to be alone and recharge my batteries. Our schools, like most institutions or offices in our country, are designed to reward extrovrets. Teachers praise the students who constantly have their hands in the air, blurting out answers to every question, while students who know the answer, but want to think longer, often go unnoticed. Bosses reward employees who jump into a project, even if they haven't thought through the consequences.

Reading Cain's book changed the way I taught. It also changed the way I thought about my own actions in social situations. I understand that I am not the person who walks into a room and goes straight to the center, hoping to engage everyone in the room. I am more content to hang at the edge, find one person, and have a good

This camp at Wright Lake on August 10, 2010, was the first night of the Green Lake Loop. Photo by Steve Gardiner

conversation with.

I explained these differences to my students. This helped them understand their own thinking and acting, and it also helped with how they understood and interacted with each other.

Most of my hiking and climbing trips are done with long-time friends or my family. I trust them in the mountains. We have a lot of fun together. While I love to share a great mountain experience, I also want to experience time alone in the natural world. The images of those days and nights alone in the mountains give me solace when I am back in school and students misbehave or meetings go too long.

Night settled in at Wright Lake. Gentle rain tapped on my tent at nine o'clock. Then quiet.

In the morning I walked to Martin Lake, a short distance to the north. I sauntered along the shore, stopping to look at the granite peaks rising behind the lake, reflected in the morning water. In the middle of the lake, a tiny rock island serves as a focal point.

The Martin Lake Basin contains four lakes which stairstep down in elevation with short sections of river connecting them. Water cascades from one lake to the next. Martin Lake, at 9,660 feet elevation is the highest, followed by Wright Lake, Spogen Lake, and Whitcomb Lake, the farthest south and lowest at 9,575 feet elevation. The gentle stairsteps make the basin a wonderful morning stroll, so after I walked to Martin Lake, I returned to Wright Lake, passed my campsite, and continued to Spogen Lake. I walked along the northeast shore and could hear the waterfall before I could see it. The falls roll over undulating bedrock, spraying water into the air. I sat on a log, listening, watching. I shot several photographs, some of my favorite that I have ever taken in the mountains. Another ten minutes walking from Spogen Lake brought me to Whitcomb Lake. The faint trail meets Whitcomb at a narrow canyon, a thin trough of water that leads to the main lake where a finger of rock stretches out into the lake. I walked out to the fingertip to be surrounded by water and morning sun.

I find it interesting how, over the years, my travels in the Beartooth Mountains have interconnected. For example, Wright Lake, where I camped on the first night of the Green Lake Loop, is two miles west of Lonesome Mountain. Many of the lakes I saw from the summit of Lonesome Mountain are the lakes I hiked past on that three-day trip. When I descended from Lonesome Mountain to Albino Lake and went out by Becker Lake, I connected with another solo trip. That trail leaves from Island Lake and goes north past Night Lake and Flake Lake.

I had walked to Flake Lake and gone around the north side to a large waterfall where a fisherman's trail leads steeply uphill. I left my backpack behind a large boulder and hiked next to the cascading river up seven hundred vertical feet to a broad bench where I visited an unnamed lake, Wall Lake, and finally Snow Lake. These are rough lakes, above the tree line and exposed to the elements. There must be some harsh days in that environment.

After visiting those three lakes, I retrieved my backpack from behind the boulder and hiked to the north end of Becker Lake, where I found an interesting campsite on a rising knob overlooking the lake. I set up camp, ate dinner, and took my food bag to hang it, a traditional precaution in bear country. I lowered the food bag over a cliff and tied the rope to a tree. I was sure it was safe, so I returned to my camp to enjoy the setting sun on the lake. Moments later, I glanced at the cliff where my food bag was hanging and a marmot had climbed down the face and was sitting on my food bag, clawing at the material. I yelled. He did not budge. I ran across the creek and up onto the cliff. The marmot left, so I pulled the food bag up and moved to a higher, steeper cliff to hang the food again. I returned to camp and within three minutes, I was running back to the cliff because the marmot had climbed onto my food bag again. What if he ate all my food? I finally went to a tall, skinny tree and managed to throw my rope over a thin branch and haul my food bag up into the tree. Problem solved. I thought.

An hour later, nearing sleep inside my tent, I could hear the snorting right outside the back of my tent. The marmot had come down off the cliff and was rooting around my campsite. I had seen the damage a marmot's teeth can do to trekking pole handles, boots, and other equipment. I did not want my tent chewed to pieces in the middle of the night. I quickly went outside with my headlamp and chased the marmot a hundred yards away from my tent. I slept through the night.

I had also done another solo hike up the next canyon to the east, which features Sheepherder Lakes. The trailhead for this trail is not well established, so I had to search to find the whisp of a trail leading into the broad valley, braided with streams. Not far past Dorf Lake, I heard a low howl that sounded like it was coming from just beyond a rise ahead of me. I crouched and slowly approached the top of the rise, catching a glimpse of a wolf moving to the left and into a side canyon.

The valley below Lower Sheepherder Lake is wider than most valleys in the Beartooths. The morning was cool, and I felt strong as I hiked to Lower Sheepherder Lake, then Upper Sheepherder Lake. I stopped for some food and water, before continuing over a rocky barrier to Snyder Lake. At the north end of Snyder Lake, I found a stream bed that made a good path into the alpine terrain above ten thousand feet. Here, the long, narrow form of Z Lake points up the valley to Promise Lake, situated in a round basin at the base of a deep, glacial cirque. No one else was in the entire valley that day. Isolation.

"When we experience awe, time slows down. It expands. We feel like we have more of it. And that sensation lifts our well-being," wrote Dan Pink in his book *When*. "Experiences of awe bring people into the present moment, and being in the present moment underlies awe's capacity to adjust time perception, influence decisions, and make life feel more satisfying than it would otherwise."

Alone, in the valley below Z Lake, I knew exactly what he was talking about.

Chapter 25

Important Moments Alone
August 12, 2001

One canyon east of Sheepherder Lakes is the Glacier Lake Trailhead. I had gone in there alone one day to hike past Mountain Sheep Lake and Mountain Goat Lake and up a U-shaped glacial valley to Frosty Lake. Just above Frosty Lake, a snow-filled couloir (a gully cut by a glacier up the face of a mountain) rises steeply above the lake to the summit of Spirit Mountain. I strapped on my crampons and pulled my ice axe out of my pack. I moved onto the snow and found the conditions perfect. With each step, my crampons found solid purchase in the snow. My ice axe offered protection if I should slip. With such solid steps, I moved easily up almost a thousand vertical feet of the couloir, reaching the unusual summit of Spirit Mountain. The summit is a triangle, with the base on the southern edge. The base of the triangle is nearly a quarter of a mile wide and the top point of the triangle is half a mile north. The whole summit area is almost perfectly flat, making it one of the largest summit areas I have seen on any mountain.

To the north of Lonesome Mountain, I completed three other solo trips over the years. One was a sixteen-mile hike up Senia Creek, across the Red Lodge Creek Plateau. In the middle of the Plateau, I stopped for several long minutes to stare into the apocalyptic remains inside the glacial cirque on Sylvan Peak where the jumble of ice blocks, massive crevasses, and avalanche rubble form one of the most chaotic landscapes in the Rocky Mountains. I descended from Red Lodge Creek Plateau and crossed the divide to Lake Mary where I saw for the first time the magnificent structure of Whitetail

Peak, named because of the two thousand-foot ice-filled couloir which runs in a straight line from top to bottom of the peak.

I returned to the Whitetail Peak area a few years later to camp at Shadow Lake. The following morning I was up and hiked over one thousand feet up to a high basin containing Ship Lake and Marker Lake. After visiting those two lakes, I took a brief sidetrip to see Bowback Lake. At Bowback Lake, I could look up and see the east face of Bowback Mountain and remember one of the hardest solo hikes I had ever completed.

That hike had started at East Rosebud Lake. A few miles above the lake, I turned south up the diminutive Snow Creek and climbed steeply up to Snow Lakes. From there, the abrupt summit of Mt. Inabnit loomed overhead. I continued to the left of Inabnit and moved into a narrow gully running up the mountain to just below the summit. I had climbed a few minutes in the gully when I heard a loud noise above. Several small rocks clattered down, followed by a rock about the size and shape of a car tire. It was rolling and bouncing down the couloir. I stepped to the right against the wall and behind a rock pillar, waiting until the falling rock had passed. Rockfall always gives me a jolt of adrenaline. It is one of the things I hate most in the mountains, perhaps because there is so little a climber can do about it. The mountain settled down, and quiet returned. I moved quickly up the couloir onto the saddle between Bowback Mountain and Mt. Inabnit. From there it was a scramble to the pointed summit of Mt. Inabnit where I had lunch and admired the stark beauty of the Beartooth Range.

As I climbed down Mt. Inabnit, I looked from the saddle to Bowback Mountain. It would be just as easy, and perhaps safer, to cross and climb Bowback Mountain, then descend the broad, sloping face down to Snow Lakes and my route back to East Rosebud Lake, so I did that. I reached my car after twelve hours of climbing, wearied, but very excited about the mountains and lakes I had seen.

These connected trips across the Beartooth Mountains are threads of a spider web linking all parts of the range to the views I saw from Lonesome Mountain.

The high plateaus of the Beartooth Mountains in Montana are covered in pristine lakes and were the highlights of several solo hiking and camping trips. Photo by Steve Gardiner

After I toured the four lakes in the Martin Lake Basin, I packed up and hiked past Trail Lake, then made the steep descent into Green Lake. There was one tent at Green Lake, but I did not see anyone nearby. Perhaps they were fishing at one of the many nearby lakes. At the northern end of Green Lake, the trail, which this far back in the mountains is infrequently used and much less-defined, splits. I turned right toward Sierra Creek, because I wanted to see three lakes up that narrow valley. I stashed my backpack inside a group of trees and followed the trail north. The creek flows over beautiful granite slabs shining in the afternoon sun. I hiked up the valley for an hour to the third lake, the small, but beautiful, Alp Lake. It was so nice to walk with no heavy pack and see such spectacular scenery. I decided to spend half an hour at Alp Lake and celebrate with a

Snickers bar. OK, there's nothing special about that, except this particular Snickers bar fell out of the bottom of my backpack when I returned from an expedition to Greenland. I brought it along on this trip to eat at a beautiful spot. Alp Lake served that role.

After I had been hiking and climbing for a couple of years, I became interested in high altitude. I want to hike up some of the fourteen thousand-foot peaks in Colorado, so I made several trips there. On two of those occasions, the friends I was supposed to climb with, for different reasons, were unable to meet me. I was left alone, so I took that opportunity to solo fourteeners, as they are called.

On the first of those trips, I drove to Leadville and found the Half Moon Campground, an excellent place to stay to climb Mount Elbert and Mount Massive, the two highest peaks in Colorado. Both have trails that are well marked, so the routes were easy to find and follow. I climbed them on back-to-back days.

The next trip, I moved a bit farther south and drove above Twin Lakes to the trailhead for La Plata. I slept in my van at the trailhead and set out at six thirty in the morning, arriving at the summit at eleven. On the way down, the snowfields I had crossed were softer from the warm sun. I had to be careful because occasionally my boots broke through the surface, an event known as post-holing, which can cause knee injuries. I made it down fine and drove that evening to Salida.

Next morning I drove west to the trailhead for Mount Shavano. I started hiking at seven and reached the summit at eleven. From there I could see another fourteen thousand-foot peak called Tabaguache nearby. It took another hour to traverse to that summit. I returned the same way I had climbed, making the roundtrip on both peaks in just over eight hours. On all five peaks, in Colorado I felt energetic, even at the higher altitudes. In fact, I enjoyed the feeling of the thin air and the challenge of breathing carefully and pacing my strides.

I left Alp Lake and returned to Green Lake. I pulled my backpack out of the trees and followed the lake shore to the point where Sierra Creek flows into Green Lake. A short distance upstream was a tent with a young couple standing outside. I hadn't talked to anyone in two days, so I walked toward their camp and greeted them. They had been camping there for three nights, fishing and relaxing. We chatted briefly, but the conversation soon turned to the dark clouds that were building in the west. The feeling in the air had changed. I decided I had better keep moving, so I said goodbye to them and returned to the point where Sierra Creek enters Green Lake.

I had heard there would be several stream crossings on the last half of the Green Lake Loop, so I had packed Teva sandals to help keep my boots dry. I changed to the sandals and waded across the stream. The cold water refreshed my feet, and I felt ready to make the hike to Lake Elaine. I hoped to walk past Lake Elaine and get to Upper Granite Lake by night.

Beyond the Sierra Creek crossing, the trail is seldom used. The faint bits of trail cross an open meadow filled with wild grasses. I could see trail for a few feet, then it disappeared. I would walk through the deep grass and find another shred of trail. I knew the general direction I needed to go, so I was not too concerned, but after more than an hour of walking this dotted line of trail, I was happy to reach the northeast corner of Lake Elaine. There I knew I would be walking across the northern end of the lake and turning south along the west side of the lake. Somewhere in the middle of the west side of Lake Elaine, the trail appeared again. Fishermen from Granite Lake had used this side more, so the trail was obvious. By this point, however, my concern was not the lack of trail, but the accumulation of thick, dark clouds. Moments later, I felt light rain. It increased quickly, and by the time I reached the south end of Lake Elaine, it was clear I needed to change my plans.

Thunder rumbled. I pitched my tent and was inside in six minutes. I took a nap during the heaviest rain, and crawled out to make dinner during a break. It rained off and on through the night.

Lying in my tent listening to the rain, I remembered the first time I had gone solo in the mountains. I was helping my father restore a house that had burned. It was decades before flipping houses was the subject of numerous HGTV shows, but we hoped to spend a few weeks during the summer fixing the problems, then put the house on the market. We had made good progress, in fact too good, because we hit a point where we could not do any additional improvements until we had an inspection. That would be at least two days. There was my opening.

As I always do, I wrote down my hiking plans and left them with family members. I drove into the Bighorn Mountains above Buffalo, Wyoming, and camped at the West Tensleep Trailhead, hoping to make a solo hike up Cloud Peak, the highest in the range. In the morning, I hiked several miles to Lake Helen and beyond to a meadow near a waterfall. I had climbed Cloud Peak twice before with friends, so I knew where I was going and what difficulties the peak would present. That background and my increased skills from the many mountaineering trips with my friends gave me confidence that I could climb it as my first solo.

I arrived at the waterfall in the early afternoon, and as I had hoped, had several hours to enjoy being in the mountains alone. I sat on a rock near the waterfall and wrote in my journal. It is interesting, some thirty-five years later, to read what I wrote:

"Last night at West Tensleep, I stood out under the stars for many long moments. There was no sound, only a million bright stars shining. The mountains, the stars, the universe live on each day throughout time whether humans observe them or not. They seem content and at peace with all around them, each mountain, each star fulfilling its role in the great play that never ends.

"I have been fortunate to discover the wilderness. So many people in today's world are too busy, too hurried to take a moment, a day, a week and fill their senses with the truth that the outdoors has to offer. I never travel in the wilderness without taking home with me a rich warm feeling which unburdens the weight of my pack and moves my boots happily along the trail.

"I think for some the effort of walking on rocky trails up and down countless hills causes them to defeat themselves before they start. They see the wilderness areas as a difficult, dangerous place not worth the effort to get there unless there is a road for their four-wheeler. It is this mental attitude that takes away the enjoyment. If they thought more of the opportunity to view unbounded natural beauty, to explore not only the meadows and mountains but their own inner being, they could gain all the riches nature offers so freely. The amount of effort involved is directly related to the perception of the person doing the activity. If a person thinks he is overextending and becoming tired, he probably will be tired and enjoy that activity less. However, if he is able to free his mind and think more of the enjoyment, his performance and perception will be greatly improved. The human mind is such a powerful thing and affects us continually in so many ways. More often than not, if our mind allows us to do something, our body is quite capable.

"The mind in the wilderness is full of imagination. Freed of the restrictions of society, the mind becomes active and happy, exploring a tremendous range of ideas and concepts it would pass over in a city. Wilderness is a catalyst to active thought. It is as if the open valleys and high peaks expand the mental powers which have been locked inside of buildings and houses."

I woke up the next morning at five and was hiking half an hour later. I kept a steady pace, stopping once to repair a sore spot on one foot. I reached the 13,167-foot summit of Cloud Peak at eight a.m. I spent a glorious hour on the summit alone. I returned to my camp by the waterfall and felt strong the entire way. What an experience. Content. I would be able to return to house renovations with a new enthusiasm.

After the night of rain at Lake Elaine, my sleeping bag and clothes were damp in the morning, so I set them out to dry. That pause gave me a chance to look around. I love the morning. The air is fresh and the sunlight touches the drops of dew on the leaves. It is a time of promise. There is a day I've never seen before, waiting to be lived. On a solo trip like this, I can spend those minutes and hours exactly as I like. I can make of the day what I want.

Because I stopped early in the rain the night before, I had two miles extra to walk on Day 3. The walk toured vast meadows in thick forests. Good hiking.

Near Granite Lake, I put the Teva sandals to good use again, crossing a series of streams that would have made a mess of my boots, and eventually, my feet. I ate lunch sitting on a log at Granite Lake, then climbed the long, uphill path back to the Clay Butte Trailhead.

The Green Lake Loop, and the many other lakes and trails I had seen from the top of Lonesome Mountain, have been a chance to experience solitude. Those moments alone make each return home more meaningful. Relationships with friends and family are clearer, stronger, brighter.

We are alone when we enter life. We are alone when we leave life. I have chosen to spend some important moments alone during my life.

Conclusion

A Moment of Overtime
February 20, 2020

In the history of time, no clock ever moved more slowly than the one that was ticking in my mind as I waited in the crowded hallway in the hospital in Moshi, Tanzania, wondering what the future held for my daughter Romney and me. An image of that moment might include a clock ten feet tall, with the second hand snapping ahead, punctuated by a bass drum at each click. The fear I felt was based on her pain, her unknown illness, but it also included a heavy dose of guilt. I was the one who had invited her to climb Mount Kilimanjaro with me. Powerful emotions like those affect our sense of reality, of the world around us.

I felt a similar ticking while I did the chest compressions on Dave Young when he collapsed in his classroom. The seconds that filled those eighteen minutes seemed endless, and were stretched further by our minds bouncing from hope to despair and back again.

The ticking took a different form and pace during my bike wreck on Molt Hill. Instead of the seconds dragging by, being expanded, they flew by at hyperspeed. My memory of the incident is a blur of color and motion, of tumbling and bouncing, of pain and confusion.

The sense of ever-moving time was far less frightening, but still urgent, in the years of dreaming about qualifying for the Boston Marathon. Seconds were important, and each second took weeks and months of preparation to earn. Then there was the moment at the start line when I came face-to-face with that dream as I took the first steps of a race held in record heat.

At the other end of the scale is the sense of time that stretches human minds beyond imagination. It is the time needed to form Jasper Cave, to drop-by-drop wear away the Pahasapa limestone into rooms and passages and fill them with stalagmites and stalactites and flowstone. It is the expansive timeframe needed for oceanic plates of the earth to slide across each other, creating faults and volcanic pressures powerful enough to push the highest mountain in the Western Hemisphere, Aconcagua in Argentina, far into the sky.

Then, between those are the moments of awe when time seemed to pause, to move not at all. As the sparkling lights of Fata Morgana danced on the illusory peaks, time was left suspended over the frozen sea ice of the Arctic Ocean off the northern coast of Greenland. The beauty of Chacraraju and Huandoy, the spectacular peaks of the Cordillera Blanca range in the Andes Mountains of Peru left time hanging and me spellbound. The energetic joy of 43-man squamish, played with no quarters, periods, or clock, simply removed time from the equation.

While adventure can be defined by activities like climbing and caving, running and cycling, it can also be expanded to included many more human endeavors. Each of us can determine what our own sense of adventure is. We can decide how we use our minutes, hours, days, and years. The adventures we choose, or that choose us, shape the way we interact with the world and how we experience time and life.

Acknowledgements

A Moment of Thanks
August 5, 2019

When Peggy and I got married in 1981, we chose "Time In A Bottle" by Jim Croce as one of the songs at our wedding. In that song, Croce talks about saving time to share it with loved ones. The words seemed important to us then, and now, thirty-eight years later, they still hold. We have had countless adventures together – traveling, hiking, biking, paddling – and have used our days well. We raised three daughters, Greta, Romney, and Denby, and they have gone on to their own adventures. I've been lucky to spend my time with the four of them in my life.

Joe Sears and John Jancik, along with too many less-frequent companions to name, have been the inspiration for and teammates on a host of memorable experiences. Dave Young helped me break into the world of teaching journalism at Jackson Hole High School. Dozens of other teachers, either when I was their student or colleague, added much to my career in education.

I want to thank Vince Long, Mike Brun, and John Jancik for reading the manuscript and providing valuable commentary. Jerry and Patti Kilts of Alsa Photography did an excellent job of preparing the photos for this book. Mike Brun created the clock graphics.

Three of these essays were previously published. "A Moment of Darkness in South Dakota" and "A Moment of Childhood Joy in Kansas" both appeared in a much shorter form in *The Christian Science Monitor*, and "A Moment of Truth in Peru" was published in a slightly different version in the anthology *Wanderlust*. A variation of "A Moment of Heat in Boston" received a gold award in the Solas Awards for Best Travel Writing sponsored by Traveler's Tales.

About the author

Steve Gardiner taught high school English and journalism for 38 years in Wyoming, Montana, and Peru. He is a National Board Certified Teacher and the 2008 Montana Teacher of the Year. He holds a Doctorate of Education degree. He has published articles in *The New York Times, The Chicago Tribune, The Christian Science Monitor, The Denver Post, Educational Leadership, Phi Delta Kappan, Education Week*, and many others. He has published four books about mountain climbing, including *Why I Climb: Personal Insights of Top Climbers* and *Highpointing for Tibet: A Journey in Support of the Rowell Fund*, as well as one book about teaching reading called *Building Student Literacy Through Sustained Silent Reading*. He has been on climbing expeditions to Alaska, Greenland, Tanzania, Peru, Bolivia, Ecuador, Argentina, Mexico, Europe, and Mount Everest. He and his wife Peggy have three daughters and live in Minnesota.

www.ingramcontent.com/pod-product-compliance
Lightning Source LLC
LaVergne TN
LVHW020927090426
835512LV00020B/3236